THE Art OF
Southern Charm

THE *Art* OF Southern Charm

PATRICIA ALTSCHUL
with Deborah Davis

DIVERSIONBOOKS

Diversion Books
A Division of Diversion Publishing Corp.
443 Park Avenue South, Suite 1008
New York, New York 10016
www.DiversionBooks.com

Front cover photo courtesy of Jenn Cady Photography (www.JennCady.com).
Back cover photo courtesy of Virgil Bunao.

Image credits: page 186 by Jenn Cady/Jenn Cady Photography; pages 4,
29, 57, 133, 191, 193 by New York Post/Splash Images; page 178 by Virgil
Bunao; page 180 by Leslie Carrier. All other photos from the author's
personal collection.

For more information, email info@diversionbooks.com

First Diversion Books edition April 2017
Print ISBN: 978-1-68230-835-6
eBook ISBN: 978-1-68230-834-9

For my wonderful parents, who taught me the art of
Southern charm, and my brilliant and accomplished son,
Whitney Sudler-Smith, who made me film it.

Contents

Introduction

One day, my son, Whitney Sudler-Smith, called to tell me he was producing a reality television show for the Bravo Network and that he wanted *me* to appear on it. This new project, called *Southern Charm*, sounded like great fun. He explained that the series would chronicle the lives, loves, comedies, dramas, and did-she/he-really-do-that social and sexual misadventures of Whitney and his very attractive friends in beautiful Charleston, South Carolina, our adopted hometown.

Whitney wanted me to appear as myself—a woman (and mother) of a certain age who would be *very* different from the show's cast of young revelers and reprobates, including captivating it-girl Cameran Eubanks, perpetually boyish Shep Rose, easygoing Craig Conover, sunny Landon Clements, and the on-again, off-again couple everyone came to love/hate, former South Carolina state treasurer Thomas Ravenel and Kathryn Calhoun Dennis. "Mom, it will take five minutes of your time," Whitney promised persuasively.

I decided to do it. Like most mothers, I cannot say no to my son, and I doubted that I would be on camera long enough to make much of an impression. After all, I was just Whitney's mother. What did I know about "throwing shade," having a "showmance," or delivering a "bitchslap"—all staple moves in the world of reality television? I figured I had nothing to lose, and that I could be myself, speak my mind, and have fun with it.

With the help of my butler, Michael (the **majordomo** of domestic affairs in my house for the past thirteen years), I showed the "Charmers" my way of doing things (which, naturally, I thought was the better way)—from mixing a perfect martini, to hosting a party, to dressing for a ball, to discussing the results of a paternity test at the dinner table (actually, *don't* try this at home!). In short order, I was surprised to find that I had become a den mother (hopefully a glamorous one) for the cast, and a lifestyle muse for the ever-growing community of *Southern Charm* viewers.

> **Majordomo:** The head steward or butler in the household of a sovereign or great noble.

That "five minutes" Whitney promised at the outset has turned into four sensational seasons, with *Southern Charm* becoming one of the most popular shows on Bravo. I mean, at my age, I'd thought I'd be sitting on my chaise, eating bonbons, and reading trashy novels, or possibly looking for a new husband—all worthy pursuits. Instead, Whitney has me working constantly. It seems that I'm always preparing, shooting, or publicizing and promoting another *Southern Charm* season.

However, my time on the show—and especially my engaged relationship with its fans—has reaffirmed something I've always known. Southern charm is more than the title of a TV show. It is a way of life that celebrates hospitality, good times, best manners, and great fun. I am a Southerner. I was born in Florida, grew up in Virginia, and subsequently lived in Washington,

DC, and New York, so I know firsthand that the differences between North and South are based on more than geography: they are different states of mind.

Northerners, let's remember, started out as Puritans in pursuit of religious freedom, so they were *not* famous for their high spirits or hijinks—while the people who settled the South descended from fun-loving courtiers and cavaliers, the playmates of kings. For them, entertaining and the pursuit of pleasure was practically a full-time job. They loved riding, shooting, drinking, playing cards, dancing, listening to music, and socializing. They were all about wine, women, and song. Actually, that pretty much describes the Southerners I know today.

If you are born and raised in the South, as I was, it gets into your blood. Even if you are not a true Southerner, you can appreciate the art of Southern charm. I didn't invent it (no, I'm not *that* old): the South has a long and legendary history of **politesse**. Fifteen-year-old George Washington, a fellow Virginian, was so concerned about being a proper Southern gentleman that he kept a list of rules in his journal. "Cleanse not your teeth with the Table Cloth Napkin Fork or Knife," "Kill no Vermin as Fleas, lice ticks…in the Sight of Others" and "bedew no man's face with Spittle," are just a few of the everyday manners the father-to-be of our country deemed important.

> **Politesse:** formal politeness or etiquette

These days we may not have to worry about fleas, lice, or spitting, but minding your manners in the twenty-first century can be a lot trickier than it was when Washington was a young man. Thanks to the show, I've discovered that all sorts of people—from *Real Housewives* aficionados to fashionistas at *Vogue*, from grandmothers to millennials, and everyone in between—want to know how to behave. Anyone who knows me, whether on the show or in real life, understands that I love to serve up advice on the rocks and with a twist. I like to have a good time and, more importantly, I want the people around me to have an even better one. Learn the rules so you can bend—and even break—them, is my philosophy. Then, let the fun begin!

I want to tell you my story and share my secrets. So, darlin', put on your caftan, prepare your dressing drink (recipes for my favorites to follow), and settle into your most comfortable chair, preferably with a warm pug nearby. You want to have a lovely life, and I'm going to show you how. Together, we will explore *The Art of Southern Charm.*

Welcome to the party!

Becoming Patricia

My paternal grandfather,
General Frank E. Dey, in
his Confederate uniform.

My Southern roots are strong. During the Civil War my paternal grandfather, Frank Edgar Dey, enlisted as a private in the Confederate Army when he was sixteen years old and moved up in the ranks to become a brigadier general. He was captured four times, including at the Battle of Vicksburg in 1863, and was wounded while fighting against General Sherman at New Hope. My grandmother was born in Alabama and she and my grandfather were married at her family plantation. When they had children of their own, they raised them deep in the heart of Texas.

My father, Walter Pettus Dey, was a brilliant and urbane young man who graduated from both the University of Alabama and Tulane University Medical School. He was a surgeon/soldier of fortune and a captain in the Navy, who traveled the world as a diplomat and a medical inspector to the Far East under President Franklin Roosevelt. He spoke several languages and his work took him to many faraway locations, such as China and Japan, where he had wonderful adventures that sounded as if they belonged in a storybook. On one memorable trip, he fought pirates from a gunboat on the Yangtze River. On another, he befriended Vajiravudh, the last king of Siam.

Father was handsome, charming, intelligent, and well read, and these attributes made him quite the catch. He had been engaged several times, but his career and travels always came first...until he met my mother. His vagabond days ended at a cotillion in Richmond, Virginia. The sight of Frances Pearl Sudler, a beautiful Yankee from Philadelphia, turned this confirmed bachelor into an ardent suitor. At the age of fifty-eight, my father married my thirty-year-old mother (she was a

Father and Mother

divorcée, something that was considered so scandalous at the time that I didn't find out until I was in my forties). Apparently my father's very Southern sister could handle the divorcée part, but she never recovered from the shock of having a *Yankee* in the family. The couple settled in Richmond, although they traveled frequently.

My parents spent a lot of time in Florida and I was born there in 1941. They called me Madelyn Patricia, but I always preferred my middle name, because it sounded less formal. By all accounts I was a good little girl. I remember being spanked and sent to my room once, and that was for tilting my chair backward at the dinner table and chipping the sideboard behind me. That seems to have been the extent of my flirtation with juvenile delinquency. I played with my dog, Happy, and my cat, Fluffy, and I rode my horse, the Grey Ghost. The big drama of my childhood

My dog, Happy, and my horse, Grey Ghost.

was that I fell off my horse and broke my hip when I was only four years old and had to wear an enormous body cast that, in photographs, looked like a medieval torture device.

Our home was beautiful and serene. There was never an argument, not even a raised voice. My parents were well matched, although their different backgrounds made for an interesting mix of parenting.

My mother was very cultivated. She spoke French, read extensively, played the piano beautifully, and excelled at embroidery and needlepoint. She was a delicate woman who frequently had

Our family in Florida

what they used to call "the vapors," meaning she would take to her bed.

My father, on the other hand, was my best companion and playmate. Other fathers went to work, but mine had retired soon after I was born, so he was around all the time and always ready for another adventure. He took me places and told me colorful stories about his travels.

I credit him with inspiring my life-long love of Southern history and literature, of all things Southern, in fact. When my father and I went to our local Episcopal church I was thrilled to sit in Robert E. Lee's

Happy times with my father.

pew. On special occasions, we traveled to George Washington's Mount Vernon to picnic on the lawn. I was in a choral group that sang Christmas carols for the last of the Confederate widows. Living in Richmond, the capital of the Confederacy, we were always conscious of the past and our family's connection to it.

My mother may have been a Yankee, but she quickly embraced all the Southern charm essentials and imparted them to me. Southern women were strong in how they dealt with life's **vicissitudes**, but they did so in a calm, gentle way—hence the term *steel magnolia*. Femininity was always emphasized. Women never left the house without being perfectly groomed, with clothes and hair in place and, if you were old enough, a light swipe of lipstick for a pop of color. My mother never once owned a pair of slacks and always wore stockings and heels.

> **Vicissitudes:**
> A change of circumstances or fortune, typically one that is unwelcome or unpleasant.

Men were gentlemen. They opened doors for ladies, stood up when they entered the room, pulled out their chairs at the table, and walked between them and the street to protect them from traffic. It all sounds so quaint in light of today's more liberated social climate, but they were lovely times. Manners, which were so important to everyone, were passed down from generation to generation, and the goal was to be gracious and hospitable.

I attended Marymount, a Roman Catholic day school for girls located on the beautiful Paxton estate in Richmond. I had to wear a dowdy uniform (picture me in *that*), and I studied with strict French nuns who taught us French, Latin, Greek, algebra, literature, penmanship, and social graces. Every day at four we gathered for *goûter*, the French version of afternoon tea that included pretend "cocktails" made of juice or tea. It was a lovely ritual that taught us a lot about comportment. We

My Marymount graduation. I'm 2nd from right.
Who wore it better?

learned what to wear, how to pour, and the proper way to hold a cup or a glass.

The nuns also emphasized the after-school "don'ts" that were so important in the conservative 1950s—no drinking, no smoking, no riding in cars with boys, and *no* public displays of affection…ever. I wonder what they would have thought of the Kardashians? I was extremely jealous of my friends at public school because they seemed to have more freedom—and infinitely more fun—than I did. Those strict nuns kept me on the straight and narrow, which was probably a good thing. Subsequently, for high school, I went to a Quaker boarding school in the Midwest, and by the time I was a senior I knew something about having a good time. I wasn't "fast," as they used to say, but I had six darling *beaux* and one particularly charming admirer who owned a convertible and a plane!

The fifties were the last golden years—a more innocent time, when we didn't take drugs, we didn't smoke or drink, and we did things in a group. We loved to dance and found it exciting to go to cotillions and parties. In a way, I think we had more fun because innocent pleasures weren't boring to us.

My beloved father died when I was eighteen and my mother and I found it difficult to stay in Richmond without him. We sailed to Europe on a beautiful ocean liner, the *Queen Mary*, and went on a classic grand tour for a year. When we returned, we settled in Washington, DC—north of where we used to live, but still close to the South—so I could attend George Washington University, and I jumped headfirst into my new life as a coed.

One night, at a party in Washington, a friend introduced me to Lon Smith, a good-looking, mature (well, five years older than me) man, who was the head of Dun & Bradstreet, a very important job for someone twenty-five years old. It was pretty close to love at first sight, because three months later we were married. When you're Southern and in your twenties, marriage is a top priority. My mother asked if I wanted a big wedding or a check, and I gave the right answer. I had been a bridesmaid at so many weddings that I was happy to do mine differently. We had a small ceremony, attended by our immediate families, and the blushing bride wore a short peach dress and a hat with a veil.

We set up housekeeping in Virginia, just a few miles from Washington, DC, and I found myself at the center of one of those newlywed sitcoms. While I commuted to school in Washington to study art history and archaeology, aspiring to work in a museum or an art gallery someday, Lon was at Dun & Bradstreet by day and went to graduate school at night for his MBA. We were so young and ambitious it never seemed to bother us that we were in constant motion. In 1963, I was thrilled to win a fellowship at the Smithsonian. I had my own desk at the Library of Congress and even learned how to read Egyptian hieroglyphics. In 1965, I graduated magna cum laude from GW, with a BA in art history. Then, I immediately started graduate school.

My classes were difficult, but a full courseload was easier than the domestic challenges that awaited me at home. Cooking dinner was one of them. I was completely inept in the kitchen— untrained, untalented, and, I dare say, *uninterested*. Like many busy young wives, I fell for the tempting photographs on the covers of the wonderful new convenience food known as the "TV dinner." I bought these miraculous inventions and waited for them to be ready, not realizing that the three-course tray had to come out of the box and be heated before it could be called "dinner." Thankfully, there was a Howard Johnson's nearby for those nights when my culinary efforts were particularly disastrous. As I recall, we spent a lot of time there.

I received my master's degree from George Washington University in 1966. I also started teaching art appreciation and a survey of Western art at GW, first as an instructor, then as an assistant professor. Standing in front of a class of 120 students, most of whom looked as if they were on their way to a sit-in, or auditioning for the cast of *Hair*, can be quite intimidating when you're only twenty-four. I teased my hair, armed myself with chic suits and low heels, as if I were channeling Jackie Kennedy, and spoke about my passion: art history. It helped that I was tall.

Even though I was the same age as some of my students, I was living a completely different kind of life. I was really kind of a bore. This was a time when young people were protesting the war in Vietnam, smoking grass, growing their hair down to their rear ends, wearing ugly sandals, and destroying brain cells with all sorts of "mind-expanding" substances. For them, it was the Age of Aquarius. For *me*, it was as if old age had set in early. I had a plan and was focused on my future. I wanted to go places, and I felt that people who didn't share my aspirations were morons. To this day, I can't stand people who are unambitious. Back then, when I looked at pictures of Woodstock, I thought it was **Armageddon.**

I worked hard at being a good teacher. Sometimes I stayed up until three in the morning preparing my lecture. The survey of Western art was usually scheduled for after lunch, and that was a problem. When I turned off the lights to show slides, some students would go to sleep...especially the fraternity boys who were forced to be there because the course was a requirement for a liberal arts degree. Still, I convinced myself that my students were taking me seriously until the day I walked into the classroom and found a note scribbled on the chalkboard. It was the handiwork of one of those shameless frat boys. They were always trying to flirt with me after class, and since some of them were pretty cute, it was a good thing—or a bad thing— that I was married. "My teacher is soft as bunny fur," one of them had written, "I think I'd like to sleep with her." A dubious compliment, but a compliment nonetheless. I smiled to myself, then gave a pop quiz that day to remind them who was boss. As you might imagine, I was a *really* tough grader.

Entertaining as they were, the pranksters in my regular classes were not my favorite students. I was more impressed by the older men and women who attended the continuing education classes I taught in the evening. Most of the men were veterans who had come back to school on the GI Bill, while many of the women were housewives. They were so dedicated and eager for knowledge. Because they were out in the world

Armageddon: In the Book of Revelation, the place where the final battle will be fought between the forces of good and evil.

working, or managing a home and keeping a family going, they really knew the value of an education. Unlike the college kids, they would never miss a class. Their time at school was too precious.

When I was promoted to assistant professor, I made it my business to develop an interesting art history curriculum for my adult students, and what I came up with was innovative at the time. I would drive to Washington and carry my projector and slides to the Veterans Affairs building, where I lectured for hours at a time. I also created a three-week international study program that took students through the major art capitals of Europe. I was always looking for ways to make art history come to life.

Lon and I chaperoned the first group of students who signed up to study abroad, which was pretty funny because we weren't much older than they were. We were off to a rocky start when we arrived in Europe only to discover that the tour company had kept the money instead of paying the places where we had reservations. Out came Lon's credit card, and it was throbbing for the entire trip. On the second or third day, one of my students, the precocious daughter of a university president, disappeared with a flight attendant for a getaway and I was a nervous wreck until she came back in one piece. The highlight of the trip was when we offered a priest a ride on our bus and he graciously arranged for us to take a private tour of the Vatican. The sight of the incredible paintings—many of which were never shown publicly—made the whole trip, misadventures and all, worthwhile.

In the midst of teaching, commuting, and running a household, I discovered that I was pregnant. At first I was taken aback. I loved my job and I didn't want to leave it. Then I realized the timing was perfect. My career was established enough for me to take a little time off for the baby and go back to work when I was ready. Meanwhile, I maintained a full schedule until I was about eight months pregnant and larger than the proverbial house.

When I look back, I can't believe I wore those awful maternity clothes. I must have been quite a sight on campus. In those days there were no fashionable outfits for women who were expecting. Pregnant women walked around in huge tents that made us look even larger than we were. One of my dresses actually had a bull's-eye to mark the baby's location. Now that I think of it, I probably should have removed the stupid bow that always seemed to decorate those shapeless garments. It was supposed to make us appear girlish and innocent, even though the "bump," as they call it now, was a dead giveaway that I'd had sex at least once. But I do think that today's expectant mothers— especially the ones wearing Hervé Leger bandage dresses—have gone a little too far in the other direction: if I can see the baby moving, the dress is probably too tight!

Ten-pound Whitney Sudler-Smith was born on June 2, 1968. I put a lot of thought into what we would call the baby because when you're working with a last name as common as Smith, you *have* to be creative. "Whitney" was the perfect choice: while it came from my mother's Mainline, Philadelphia, side of the family, it is also very Southern. Sudler was my mother's maiden name, and it was a nice alliterative companion to Smith. I thought that the hyphen added a touch of drama and made it a different name. There's no other Whitney Sudler-Smith.

Whitney was the most beautiful baby ever born—I'm not saying that because I'm his mother—and he had a personality to match. He was a big baby, so he acted more mature than the typical scrawny newborn. He slept through the night and gurgled and cooed when he was awake, just like the Gerber baby. He was always happy and gregarious, which made motherhood

Whitney with his proud and adoring parents.

so easy and enjoyable for me. I hadn't spent much time around children, so I took the academic approach and read lots of books about bringing up baby. I remember dressing him in starchy little outfits with pleats and monograms (you can never have too many monograms), and just when he looked picture-perfect, he'd spit up all over himself, the way most babies do.

Right after Whitney was born, Lon had to attend a business training program in New York City, so we sublet an apartment on the Upper East Side for four months. Of course, there were parks in the neighborhood, but my favorite outing was pushing the carriage to Bloomingdale's, the most popular department store in Manhattan at the time. It was a giant bazaar, filled with everything you ever wanted. I spent hours going from floor to floor. I was the thinnest I've ever been because Whitney was huge, and lifting him was like carrying barbells around all day. It was a fitness routine that rivaled any trip to the gym.

Back in Virginia, we moved into a house in Falls Church and hired a housekeeper. But I soon found that Whitney's grandparents—Lon's mother and my mother—were so devoted to their grandson that I rarely needed babysitters. They wanted to be with him constantly and I was all for it because they were such a good influence. I raised Whitney exactly the way my mother and father raised me. I never hold back when behavior is unacceptable, so Whitney was always being reminded, "don't slurp," "stand up straight," and such. Honestly, Lon was such a gentleman that Whitney learned by his example. He saw his father open my car door, or stand when I entered the room, and eventually it became second nature for him to do the same. Even as a little boy, he knew to say "yes, ma'am," and "no, sir," to adults—he may still do it today.

Everything was very *Father Knows Best* and *The Adventures of Ozzie and Harriet* in the continuing sitcom of my life, until Lon and I realized we were growing apart. Actually, we were so young when we married that maybe we were finally growing up. After fourteen lovely years of marriage, there was no acrimony between us—just a sense that we were moving in different directions. Our separation and divorce were completely civilized and our main concern was always our son.

When I think back, we were way ahead of our time. I even had a "manny," a male nanny, to help. At this point, Whitney was attending school in Georgetown, so Lon and I each set up a household there and established a seam-

Whitney having a very serious conversation with Santa.

less coparenting schedule. I had Whitney on Mondays and Tuesdays, Lon on Wednesdays and Thursdays, and we alternated weekends. We made sure that he had everything he needed in both places, so he would always feel as if he were "home." More importantly, Lon and I spoke frequently and were pleasant, respectful, and harmonious. There was nothing **pernicious** about our relationship at the time, and we're still that way after all these years. I couldn't have picked a better father for Whitney, who never had to feel divided about his feelings for his parents.

Pernicious: having a harmful effect, especially in a gradual or subtle way.

The fact that Whitney was thriving and my domestic affairs were in order enabled me to focus on an exciting new career path. I loved being out and about in the art world. Recently I had transitioned from being a professor to an art advisor—a professional who connects collectors with the works of art they hope to acquire. It is a fast-paced, high-stakes profession that requires a good eye, a cool head, and strong relationships.

I partnered with a top art scholar in a company we called Arcadia, dealing in the rarest and most desirable nineteenth-century American paintings and watercolors. I would find the work (this was a time when it was still possible to make great discoveries—I'd get a call from someone saying, "My aunt has a Martin Johnson Heade, can you come take a look at it?"), and then I would have it authenticated. After we built a major collection for an important client, other collectors and museums wanted me to find acquisitions for them.

Paintings have taken me everywhere, from dinners at Buckingham Palace and Versailles to the White House, from the most hush-hush private collections to galleries and auction houses all over the world. The 1980s were very good to me. I met the most interesting people, including barons, senators,

Enjoying polo at a château outside of Paris.

astronauts, and movie stars, and made a lot of money, enough to afford a wonderful lifestyle in Georgetown.

What a lovely life we had. Whitney was a terrific child, smart, creative, talented, and great company. He was popular and athletic at Georgetown Day School, where he played tennis, baseball, and golf, and he often went whitewater rafting with his father. He's always been a great writer and illustrator. I still have some of the books he made. He and his friends started a newspaper for students in Washington, telling them where to go for the best movies, music, hot spots, and, of course, girls. He was trained to play classical guitar—something he still does every day.

After graduating from high school, Whitney attended George Washington University, my alma mater, where he excelled. Once he had his BA, he decided to go to Europe. I was hoping he would end up at the London School of Economics, but that was the last thing Whitney wanted. He studied at Oxford for the summer. Then he moved to Paris, where he studied French literature, and traveled all over Europe. My son was always very independent and managed to create a cosmopolitan life for himself—in a foreign country, no less.

After I divorced, I could have remarried several times, but being a good mother to Whitney always came first, my career came second, and having fun came third. I never dated when Whitney was in the house—it wasn't that important to me. Then, while he was in England and France, I started rethinking my priorities. In 1989, a friend introduced me to Edward Fleming. He was a doctor, a prominent psychiatrist who founded the Psychiatric Institutes of America. On top of that, he was movie-star handsome, charming, an accomplished yachtsman, and a direct descendant of Robert E. Lee. He quickly swept me off my feet and onto his magnificent new motor yacht, the *Silver Cloud*. After we were married, it was anchors aweigh for the next year and a half, as we sailed from place to place.

The boat was beautiful, I'll give it that. It had all the comforts and appointments of a luxurious home, and then some—a fireplace, paintings, antiques, silver, china, and comfortable furniture. The crew consisted of a captain from Brittany, a chef from Paris, and two deckhands. We'd dock in a wonderful location and spend time exploring. The *Silver Cloud* had everything, including bicycles and two dinghies, and sometimes we rented a car or a helicopter. Being on a yacht was a lovely way to spend time and was certainly the most civilized way to travel.

However, when you live on the water you lose all contact with the world. I assumed we would end up on **terra firma** at some point, especially since my mother was ill and I wanted to be near her. But Ed tried to isolate me from everyone—and everything—I loved. The **coup de grâce**? The moment that he proposed we

Terra firma:
dry land; the ground as distinct from the sea or air.

Coup de grâce:
an action or event that serves as the culmination of a bad or deteriorating situation.

renounce our American citizenship and move to Ireland for tax purposes. I love being an American and had no interest in becoming a tax exile. I decided it was time to get off the boat, even if it meant another divorce. It takes a lot of strength to walk away from a marriage, and let me tell you, it is very hard—no, almost impossible—to serve papers to someone who lives on a yacht and is always in motion. The process took a few years.

Meanwhile, I was back in Virginia, taking care of my ailing mother and contemplating the next direction my life should take. In May 1993, I accepted an invitation to a highly anticipated event in the Washington art world, the reopening of James McNeill Whistler's Peacock Room at the Smithsonian. I had no idea how important that day would be for me. There, I ran into Arthur Altschul, one of my favorite former clients, and a friend for twenty years.

Ahh…Arthur. He was the last of his breed: brilliant, charismatic, a great businessman, and a true gentleman with infallible taste and the best sense of humor. He was quite the luminary: a partner at Goldman Sachs, a philanthropist, a major art collector, and on top of everything else, a divine human being.

I always admired Arthur and suspected he felt the same way about me. But as

The incomparable Arthur Altschul.

fate would have it, whenever we were together, one of us was inconveniently married to someone else. This time was different. Arthur told me that he was divorced, that he had been trying to call me, and that he would love to take me out. On the spot, he invited me to come to New York for an event at the Metropolitan Museum of Art.

I accepted and we spent a wonderful evening together. When Arthur impetuously said, "Please stay," I took him seriously. I viewed our sudden romance as an adventure, and I'm all about having adventures. At first I went back and forth to Virginia. Then we married and settled into domestic bliss at a very high level. Arthur would go off to Goldman Sachs or his family investment firm to be a mogul every day, while I oversaw the many moving parts of our private life. Arthur owned an apartment on Fifth Avenue and Overbrook Farm in Connecticut, and managing these enormous residences (and the staff that went with them) was like running a giant hotel.

The apartment, which had been decorated by three previous wives, was in need of a serious intervention. Armed with tear sheets, ideas, and wish lists, I called the one and only Mario Buatta, the acclaimed interior designer I had admired for many years. When I showed him my huge file of "Mario" clippings, Mario joked that I knew more about him than he did. Working together on this project was the beginning of a long-standing collaboration and a great friendship.

Then there was Arthur's fabulous art. He had an important collection and he loved showing it. Groups came through the house to admire the great paintings—works by Georgia O'Keeffe, Winslow Homer, Mary Cassat, Childe Hassam—any of which would have been at home in a museum. When Arthur wasn't busy running his financial empire, he was a very active board member at several major institutions, including the Metropolitan Museum.

I knew how much he appreciated beauty, so I always surrounded myself with my prettiest and most amusing girlfriends. I also planned parties that he would enjoy. My only rule was that nothing could be stodgy or boring; that's where my Southern upbringing came in handy.

Early on in our relationship, Arthur asked me to host a holiday event for his partners at Goldman Sachs. When I think holiday, I think Christmas. I asked Arthur if I could unpack my decorations and go to town. Even though he was Jewish, he was all for it (and honestly, it never dawned on me that Christmas wasn't a part of everyone's holiday celebration). I ordered a gigantic Christmas tree and covered it with so many lights that we shorted the electricity in the apartment building. In addition to my collection of ornaments, I placed crossed Confederate flags at the top of the tree, an innocent attempt to pay homage to my Southern roots. Finally, out came my mechanical singing iguana, belting out "Feliz Navidad" at the push of a button. Instead of the usual Goldman Sachs party, it was a Santa-lollapalooza!

As the guests arrived, I realized that I was an **anomaly** in this group. Most of the wives (and their husbands, for that matter) were Yankees through and through. I never felt so Southern in my life. I'm sure they thought I was a Southern eccentric—or a foreigner. My mother always referred to people whose background she didn't understand as "foreign." After the culture shock passed, we all became best friends.

Anomaly: something that deviates from what is standard, normal, or expected.

It was the nineties, so the caterer was all for offering something trendy and metropolitan, like sushi, which I never eat, but this Southern girl knew that the quickest way to a guest's heart is via pork. Yes, pork, as in good old ham and bacon. "Raise the hoof" if you want to win friends and influence people! We served Smithfield ham (irresistibly flavorful because the pigs are fed a diet of peanuts), pigs in blankets with French's mustard, and strips of caramelized bacon. A shrimp tower, deviled eggs, Krispy Kreme donuts, and other classic Southern treats rounded out the menu and made for an evening no calorie- or carb-counting New Yorker would ever forget. Arthur loved it, and so did all his partners. They thought they'd gone to pig heaven, and the food was gone in twenty minutes.

Arthur and I had been married for about five years when his health started to decline. He was such a vital and vibrant man that he refused to allow illness to slow him down for a minute. He still enjoyed going out and having a very active social life. We never missed an opening at a museum, an auction house, or an art gallery, or a good party—at home or abroad. When we stayed home it was at Southerly, the beautiful waterfront estate we acquired in Oyster Bay, New York.

Beautiful Southerly.

My favorite you-can't-keep-Arthur-down story happened when we were flying to Paris on the Concorde to spend Thanksgiving with friends. About an hour into the flight, after the meal had been served, there was the sound of a big boom. The plane started shaking and losing velocity. I was paralyzed, figuring we were headed for the ocean. Arthur, who was sitting in front of me, starting ringing for help. I was terrified that he was having a heart attack, so I called out, "Arthur, are you all right?" Very calmly, he turned around and answered, "I'm fine. My dinner roll fell on the floor." He was ringing for an attendant to pick it up. The plane made it to Paris (after a hellish eight hours because it had blown an engine). Fabulous Arthur never lost his composure, not for a moment.

Arthur passed away on Saint Patrick's Day in 2002. I was devastated to think that I would never see this wonderful man again. We came to each other late in life and had so little time together. I was inconsolable. The only person who could cheer me up was my dear friend, fashion icon André Leon Talley. André is brilliant, outrageous, and imperious. After the funeral, he came to Southerly for a weeklong visit and took charge in his inimitable way, insisting that we put on our caftans, eat pizza, and watch way too much television. He was a wonderful distraction…until he left, and then it was time for me to accept my new status: widow.

Dismantling Arthur's estate, starting with the New York apartment, kept me busy and distracted. I missed Whitney, who was living in Los Angeles, taking filmmaking courses and writing screenplays. I've discovered that when Whitney sets his mind to something, it happens. Before long, he was actually making films. His first indie features were *Bubba and Ike*, a comedy about rednecks (not sure where he learned about that subject), followed by *Torture TV* (another interesting choice), starring Danny Huston.

I stayed on at Southerly for six years after Arthur died, and eventually there were some happy times. I rescued two adorable minihorses, named them Beauregard and Maggie, and built a ministable and a paddock for them so they would have a proper home.

Speaking of proper homes, in 2004, I was dreading the process of finding a new butler for Southerly. I know, it sounds like a high-class problem, but identifying the right person to take charge of domestic affairs for a place that large is no easy feat.

Mario Buatta whispered in my ear that Mrs. A.C. Bostwick, a classic grande dame who maintained a huge estate in Old Westbury, New York, had passed away and that one of her prized employees would be on the job market. But not for long, he warned. Michael Kelcourse, Mrs. Bostwick's formidable butler, would be snapped up as soon as word got out that he was available. Desperate socialites were already circling the wagons. I followed Mario's advice and moved with indecent speed. I met with Michael immediately and persuaded him to come work for me, even as he was finishing his responsibilities in the Bostwick household.

Best thing I could have done. As anyone who watches *Southern Charm* knows, Michael is a consummate professional: smart, skilled, and with impeccable taste. Best of all, he has a killer sense of humor—dry as my favorite martini. I became "Mrs. A," and Southerly was at its best. But with every passing year, the Long Island winters were getting colder and harder, and I started dreaming about having a place down South.

For some people, the obvious choice would be Palm Beach, but, honestly, I've never, ever, been a Palm Beach person. It's fun to visit, but it's not really Southern. It's basically fake Regency in terms of architecture, and everyone I know goes there in the winter, so it's a lot like a "little New York," but with palm trees. If I went to a party I'd know everyone, which can be unexciting. And I'd never find a restaurant that served fried chicken and hush puppies.

Michael, the butler, with a dog and a cocktail—perfection!

Where was my dream destination? There was only one way to find out. With Michael at the wheel, I started taking road trips to various places in the South. I was a younger version of "Miss Daisy," driven from location to location, trying to imagine myself in a new home. Although Michael was born in Michigan and has a high tolerance for cold weather, he was game to relocate. We explored properties in Virginia, Georgia, and the eastern shore of Maryland. Like Goldilocks, I was on a quest for the place that was not too big, not too small, but "just right." Then I came to Charleston.

The cobblestone streets, the beautiful vistas of water along the Battery, the flowers, the food, the architecture, the overwhelming sense of tradition, genealogy, and history wherever you go (just like my beloved Richmond, Virginia)…what didn't I like about Charleston? I'm not alone in my affection for this great city. In 2016, based on voter response, *Travel & Leisure* ranked Charleston number one on their list of the World's Best Cities. Not number one in the country, but in the *world*, beating out places like Paris and London.

I looked at six or seven houses in Charleston, and I even considered buying a plantation. But when I discovered that you could have an alligator in heat turn up on your front porch, I decided that plantation living was not for me. The first time I set eyes on the Isaac Mikell House was during a driving tour of Charleston, when I was trying to figure out what kind of a house I wanted. I always loved houses with columns because they fulfilled my *Gone with the Wind* fantasy. The Mikell House was not for sale at the time, but I told my realtor, "*That's* what I want."

A year later, the house popped up on the market and I immediately flew down with Mario Buatta to take a look. The house was built in the 1850s by Isaac Mikell, a wealthy planter, as a gift for his third wife, Martha Pope, who must have been very impressed by her husband's taste and generosity. It is a beautiful combination of classic Roman revival and Italianate architecture with large columns, intricate decorative touches, and walled gardens. Even though it is located in a busy part of Charleston, the property has an enchanted, otherworldly feel, as if it were a country estate. In fact, the proper name for it is an "urban plantation," a rarity in real estate.

The house had deteriorated. For thirty years it had served as the Charleston Free Library. Subsequently, it was divided into two residences. It was dark and poorly decorated, but Mario saw through these problems and said that the house had beautiful bones. It still had great moldings, for example. But it needed to be put back together.

Michael recalls that I said (maybe too optimistically) that the house just needed a little painting. I must have succumbed to momentary denial, or insanity, because I knew it would take a tremendous amount of work to restore the place to its former splendor. We discovered that every system needed to be replaced or restored. I searched my heart and decided I was up to the challenge. I had found my Tara and I was ready to come back to the South. Let the renovation begin! I sold Southerly, placed my furniture in storage, packed up Michael and the animals, put Mario Buatta on speed-dial, and moved to Charleston to turn my dream into a reality.

It was a monumental job. Thankfully, I found a great architect named Lewis Graeber to oversee the project. I was on site every step of the way, living like a squatter in whatever part of the house wasn't under construction. All I had was a bed, a lamp, and a bridge table, which I moved from room to room. I was surrounded by twenty-five to thirty construction workers, who managed to fill 125 dumpsters. Mario flew down about

ten times to coax the house back to life. My beautiful bathroom, which so many of you have admired after seeing it on the show and in magazines, started out as a cavernous room with a rusty sink and an old toilet. Mario waved his magic wand and transformed it into the fantasy room it is today, complete with my infamous Marie Antoinette–like *cabinet*, because I vowed I would never again look at an unsightly toilet.

Of course, the gardens and the pool needed extensive work, too. Everything took time, energy, patience, and buckets of money. But when the renovation was finished, the house was everything I ever wanted.

And I was thrilled with my new hometown. My New York friends always thought the South was all about Gator Boys and Honey Boo Boo. They were amazed by how charming and beautiful Charleston is—and some of them have followed me here.

Michael, who is a Yankee, after all, could not get over how everybody on the street said "Good morning" and "How are you?" He thought it was bizarre behavior, until he got used to it. There is a graciousness, a warmth, and a sense of hospitality in Charleston that is quintessentially Southern.

In 2008, I opened my doors to new friends, new adventures, and, of all things, a movie camera. Whitney's film career was really taking off and I was fascinated when he told me about his new project. He wanted to make a documentary about the fashion designer Halston. I love fashion, and I used to wear lots of Halston (I met him once in New York), so I thought it was a great idea. I was also intrigued by the era. I had never experienced Studio 54. I was too busy working in the 1980s, and Washington, DC, is not exactly the party capital of the world. I wanted to know more about Halston and his glamorous scene and I imagined other people would feel the same way.

Whitney asked me to be in the film, which he titled

Ultrasuede (after Halston's favorite fabric). I said yes—and there I was, dressed in what I hoped was slenderizing black, wearing my signature sunglasses, and raising a glass to his future success. Much to my surprise, I was completely relaxed. The whole process felt natural to me. And here I am now...a regular on one of Bravo's most popular series and the proud winner of the 2016 Bravo Susan Lucci Award for Best Performance in a Reality Show. Then there's the ultimate compliment, a tweet from the fabulous Lady Gaga: "Patricia on #SouthernCharm, like lookin' in the damn mirror. Cheers queen." From the convent school to Andy Cohen's clubhouse (can I go on record as saying I have a crush on the fabulous Andy Cohen?), my life has been quite a journey. And, honestly, "reality" gets more interesting every day!

How to be Lovely

We hear so many platitudes about beauty—that it is in the eye of the beholder; that it is only skin deep; that it comes from within; that it doesn't buy happiness…no, wait. That's *money*. All true (except for the part about money). I happen to believe that one thing above all others makes a woman (or a man, for that matter) beautiful: confidence. The French call it *bien dans sa peau*, or being comfortable in your own skin.

I think that you should accept your uniqueness and not try to follow fashion or trends, because they can backfire and make you look ridiculous. I've survived many fashion fads… just barely. When I was growing up in the South in the 1950s, we wore bobby socks, saddle shoes, twin sets, poodle skirts, cinch belts, neck scarves, and crinolines—lots of them—that had to be starched with sugar water. They made us look like fat ballerinas! Then there were the linebacker shoulderpads from the 1980s. What were we thinking? Through it all, I've learned that I look and feel my best when I am the best possible version of myself, inside and out.

Back in '02, (you probably think that's 1902), nobody wore extensions, nobody puffed up their lips, and nobody had fake boobs or big butts. I mean if you had big boobs, you were considered **bovine**. We used to wear minimizers and girdles to camouflage all of the above. Now people buy spillage. I think fake body parts are kind of scary. There were no breast or booty implants in my day, and the world may have been a better place as a result. So let me offer my thoughts on diet, makeup, hair, wardrobe, and everything else that goes into achieving a look that is classically glamorous.

Bovine: of, relating to, or affecting cattle.

Diet

It probably seems strange for a Southerner to offer advice about diet because we are not famous for being the healthiest eaters. I consider fried chicken, pimento cheese, ham and biscuits, Krispy Kreme donuts, and candy corn to be in a food group all their own—and I will never give them up. So, the battle to maintain my waistline is one that never ends. Name the fad diet and I've been on it, hoping to make those dreaded extra pounds disappear.

All fad diets work, until they don't. I've discovered that the best way to manage my weight is the Mediterranean approach. I eat healthy, organic food. That means seafood that is not farmed, organic chicken, grass-fed beef, and lots of vegetables. I stay away from fruit unless it is high in fiber. My favorites are raspberries, blackberries, and pears. Michael frequently undermines my best efforts by whipping up irresistible temptations like his famous sweet potato casserole, and I've been known to roll over and play dead for a divine box of chocolates. But I try to control myself. And I drink plenty of alkaline water for hydration and digestion.

One of my favorite vegetables is the artichoke. It seems to have gone out of style, and I can't imagine why, because it is truly a crowd-pleaser at lunch or dinner. An artichoke with sauce sounds like a sinful combination, but they're so fibrous, and they take so long to eat, that you're probably burning more calories than you consume. That's why they're so popular with supermodels. Michael steams them to perfection and serves them on special plates, with a ramekin of melted butter on the side.

Michael's Steamed Artichokes

Trim the tops and bottoms to make them level and steam upside down for an hour. Mrs. A likes melted butter. I like browned butter with lemon, shallots, and crushed capers. Balsamic vinegar is another favorite of mine, with a drop of honey to lessen the bite. I also like a classic Béarnaise.

And here's the proper way to eat an artichoke:

◈ Artichokes are always eaten with the fingers.
◈ Remove one petal at a time and dip the base into sauce.
◈ Delicately pull through slightly clenched teeth to remove the soft, pulpy part.

◈ Discard on plate, pull off another petal, and
   start again.
◈ Spoon out the fuzzy choke at the base, discard,
   and eat the soft center that remains.

By the way, it is perfectly proper to eat asparagus with your fingers, too, as long as it is firm and undressed. If a sauce is served, Emily Post recommends using a knife and fork. When eating finger foods, a crystal finger bowl filled with water and lemon is a nice touch at the end of the meal. Just make sure you set an example for your guests so no one makes the **faux pas** of picking it up and drinking it—I think one of Whitney's friends did that!

Faux pas: an embarrassing or tactless act or remark in a social situation.

I also think it is important to have healthy snacks. Sometimes when I'm working, Michael surprises me with a small tray of cheese and crackers and water—an instant pick-me-up. At night, I like to keep dried figs by my bed, or an individual bag of SmartPop popcorn.

But the most important meal of the day—and my personal favorite—is breakfast. Look, I'm lucky. It's no secret that Michael delivers my breakfast on a tray each morning. I sit in bed, in my beautiful room, with an exquisite arrangement of coffee (usually a skim latte), the breakfast dish du jour (steel-cut oatmeal, high-fiber cereal, or one of Michael's special eggs), my daily lineup of newspapers, including the *New York Times*, the *New York Post*, the *Financial Times*, my iPad, and my iPhone. This is my time to reenter the world, to read the news and my emails, and to determine my goals for the day.

You don't need a Michael of your own to make it happen (although it does help). Orchestrate your own pleasant awakening each day, even if it means getting up a little earlier. Set aside the time to have that good cup of coffee, to scan the headlines, and to eat something on pretty china. It can be cereal or a piece of toast (or how about one of those Krispy Kremes?), if you're pressed for time. The point is to pamper yourself and to experience a mindful start to the new day. You may not be able to control anything that happens from this moment on, but you will feel fortified by a brief calm before the daily storm.

On days when you have time to indulge, try one of these classic breakfast dishes. At the moment, I'm loving Michael's coddled egg, another throwback recipe that deserves a revival. To make this dish you need a special egg coddler, which is a porcelain cup with a lid. Royal Worcester, the china company that claims to have invented the dish in the nineteenth century, still makes lovely egg coddlers today.

Michael's Coddled Egg

- ¼ teaspoon butter
- 1 egg
- Salt and pepper

Butter the inside of the egg coddler and metal lid. Break an egg into the cup. Season to taste with salt and pepper. Screw the lid firmly. Stand the egg coddler up to its neck in a pan of boiling water. Simmer for 7–8 minutes. Lift from water, open. And eat with a spoon.

Exercise

I think a little exercise goes a long way. Do Southern women work out? When I think of hardbodies, I see Northerners setting their alarms for 5 a.m. and getting up in the dark to race off to the gym. You'll never find me doing that, although I've always been athletic. When I was in school I played on a champion field hockey team, loved to ride horses, swam, and played tennis. We didn't go to gyms to work out, we actually went out and did things. Movement was a part of our lives. I still have that approach to exercise today: of course, walking is the best thing we can do for ourselves. So keep it natural instead of overdoing it. I know young people who are getting joint replacements, whereas I—who never subjected myself to excessive exercise—have not been troubled by that...yet. We'll see.

Exercising mermaid style at Weeki Wachee Springs in Florida.

Gilding the Lily

In my day, women never went outside unless they were made up to perfection. Today, women run around in their sweatsuits, with their faces au naturel, and their hair uncombed, and they look just ghastly. When you look like you've just been shot out of a cannon you can't be attractive to the opposite sex, or any sex for that matter. But, before you can even think about when and how to enhance your appearance, you must follow the golden rule for aspiring Southern belles: stay out of the sun. My mother impressed upon me that I should never, ever bake in the sun, and that was at a time when young people covered themselves in baby oil and used reflectors for that crispy, brown, shake-and-bake look.

The rule is to wear sunblock at all times. One of the inventors of sunblock was a Southerner, a Floridian named Benjamin Green. We have him to thank for our first defense against wrinkles, freckles, and more serious skin conditions. Part of the reason I look younger than my years—or so I've been told—is that I scrupulously avoid the sun. Short of carrying a parasol (and what would be wrong with that?), I always protect my face and hands. Even when I go swimming, I do it at the end of the day, when there are no harsh rays. As a result, I have fewer wrinkles than my friends who are forty.

I'm happy being pale, but I fully endorse using makeup to work in concert with Mother Nature. When I was young, the one product we were allowed was a lipstick called Tangee. Its claim to fame was that it looked orange in the tube, but, magically, it changed to a pinkish color on the lips. I hear some places still have it in stock. It would be fun to try it now. And back then, all the girls used cake mascara. As I recall, we would spit on it, mix it with the brush, and apply it to our lashes. It sounds gross now, but it really worked and in a funny way felt very Parisian.

Makeup is important, but you need a light touch. You don't want to look like the Whore of Babylon. In case you don't know she is, the Whore of Babylon was "the mother of harlots and abominations of the Earth" in the Bible's Book of Revelation. Apparently, she was a flashy, overdone sort, with tacky makeup and loud clothes—*not* someone you want to emulate. When I wear makeup, I like to use a soft pink lipstick—something like MAC's Mineralize Rich Lipstick in "Be Fabulous," with a touch of gloss, Chanel's "Healthy Glow" foundation, and Charlotte Tilbury "Cheek to Chic" blush.

My favorite throwback beauty technique is curling my eyelashes. I started using an eyelash curler when I was in boarding school and I still do it every day. Always curl *before* you apply mascara for a natural, wide-eyed look.

These days, I am blessed with Karen Thornton, a fabulous makeup artist who does my face for the show, and I am the happy recipient of her best insider tips. She told me about my favorite, must-have-on-a-desert-island tool: the Beauty Blender, a sponge that creates a subtle, polished effect and makes me look nice and blurry around the edges. Even I can't guess my age.

I have a proper dressing table, positioned in a place that gets good, natural light, where I keep my makeup and beauty supplies. It feels very "I enjoy being a girl" to sit down at a dressing table (preferably with a dressing drink). My daily supplies, such as pencils, camouflage sticks, mascara, and the like, are laid out on a silver tray. I keep my brushes in mint julep cups and I have them washed daily to avoid bacteria. I can say with certainty that my fingers never touch my face because that's a surefire way to spread germs. Instead, I use pads, cotton balls, brushes, Q-tips—anything sterile.

I take off every stitch of makeup at night with Neutrogena facial wipes, Clinique Non-Oily Eye Make-Up Remover, a gentle face cleanser, and a few times a week I use a gentle exfoliant to get rid of dead skin cells. Then I moisturize and repeat the next day. I recommend having a daily routine. The more regularly you do something, the easier it is to remember to do it. But I believe that your skin care regime should be prescribed by a dermatologist—I have three: Dr. Marguerite Germain in

Charleston; Dr. Dennis Gross in New York; and Dr. Harold Lancer in Los Angeles. A dermatologist can analyze your skin and recommend the right products for your skin type—think of skin care as being medical rather than cosmetic. And don't forget to get a full-body exam once a year.

As for any other kinds of (ahem) "enhancements" to help turn back the clock…I'm game as long as they're subtle improvements. Some plastic surgery can be a boon, but you don't want to look as if you've been through a wind tunnel, where everything is stretched so tight you're begging for slack. Cosmetic surgery and injections should not make a person look like a reject from the cast of *La Cage aux Folles*. And I'm all for trying new procedures. I called in Dr. Berger, our veterinarian, when Siegfried and Roy were having leg problems, and he offered to use his acupuncture needles to give me a minifacelift. I was enthusiastic…until he told me there could be no sex—or alcohol—for an hour after!

Lately I've started doing cryofacials, which involves going to the dermatologist and having liquid nitrogen vapors applied to my face and neck. The procedure stimulates collagen and decreases wrinkles. I brought Landon with me the last time I went because she was concerned about sun damage. It was a fun thing to do together.

I'm also a big believer in dental hygiene. If you are making an investment in your appearance, put your money where your mouth is. Clean, white teeth will always make you look pretty and young. It is so important to take care of your teeth. Explore straightening, bonding, whitening…anything you can do for a better smile. I practically live at the dentist's office. I have a cleaning every three months.

The Ritual Bath

One of my favorite indulgences is taking a relaxing bath before I go to bed. I'm fortunate to have a fireplace and a television in my bathroom, but there are other ways to create a luxurious spa experience. I light candles, fill the tub with water—not too hot, because it causes dry skin—and add a generous amount of Deep Sleep bath oil.

After a long soak, I dry off and apply Epicuren Discovery Orange Blossom After Bath moisturizer. My indulgences continue in the bedroom. Before I get into bed, I spray my pillows with "Sleep" pillow mist by Bath & Body Works. The scent is soothing and it covers all traces of dog treats (Chauncey, I'm speaking to you). I sleep on a silk pillowcase I obtained from my dermatologist. The Branché Charmeuse Case miraculously prevents wrinkles, preserves your hairstyle, and feels wonderful. My windows have curtains and blackout shades and I've been known to wear an eye mask. A good night's sleep makes me look and feel younger.

I think that long hair is youthful and I've kept mine that way for decades, although there has been the occasional mishap. When I was a debutante, my grandmother decided a perm was what I needed. The fumes were like formaldehyde—not that I know what that smells like—and the end result was awful, like the bride of Frankenstein. I was totally undone by the whole experience. You can be sure there are no pictures of me at my deb party.

Since that **debacle**, I've taken my cue from Truman Capote. He said that if a woman maintains the same hairstyle over the years, she will never age. I hope he's right. I think this philosophy applies to hair color, too. If you were a brunette, stay with your natural color as long as

> **Debacle:**
> a sudden and ignominious failure; a fiasco.

you can remember it! Too many women drift into being blonde or redhead as they get older, when their skin tone is screaming for a more authentic shade. If you're not a natural blonde, think twice about adding too many highlights; they can strip your hair and make it dry and brittle.

And don't forget about your eyebrows: they frame your face and should be shaped properly (and tinted if they're going gray). A well-defined arch can have the impact of a facelift, without the pain or the price! For all things eyebrow, Anastasia of Beverly Hills has every product you need to achieve perfect brows.

Best Dressed

Yes, we're influenced by fashion insiders, celebrities, and even friends whose taste we admire, but your goal should be to develop signature looks that are flattering, comfortable, and, most importantly, expressive of who *you* are and how you live. With the exception of my self-confessed caftan addiction, I curate my wardrobe. I believe in editing what you have. I don't buy trendy clothes and I wear what I have forever. I'd rather add one really good piece to my collection every year than have an excess of lesser "options." If you think of your wardrobe as falling into two broad categories—casual and dressy—and buy and organize accordingly, your choices will be straightforward.

Casual

My casual clothes are variations on a uniform. I'm tall, five foot nine, and long-legged, so most days you'll find me wearing trim black pants and a fitted black tee topped with a short or a long cardigan. Alternately, I pair my pants with a crisp white shirt. You will never see me in ripped jeans. I don't know who invented them, but they make a woman look as if she has been dragged through a thorny hedge backward. My outfit may be subdued, but my earrings, usually by David Webb, are large, bright, and colorful statement pieces, and I tend to wear the same ones every day. On the rare occasion when I need to look dressier during the day, I wear a sleeveless dress with a matching coat and low heels.

Cocktails and Evenings Out

For cocktail parties and other evenings out, the one piece every woman should have in her fashion arsenal is the little black dress. If you want to do some research, read *The Little Black Dress* by my dear friend André Leon Talley, the most charming, brilliant, and discerning man ever. The book shows you different styles and silhouettes, and you can use that information when selecting your own LBD, at whatever price point is appropriate for you.

In the book, André talks about two of *my* black dresses. The first time we met, I was wearing an Yves Saint Laurent *Le Smoking* tuxedo coatdress, one of my favorite choices for evening. André loved it, too, but he was even more impressed by what he spied in my purse. "When I met Mrs. Patricia Altschul for the first time at a black-tie dinner in Paris, she wore this

My dinner with André.

dress, and when she opened her elegant black envelope evening bag, I noticed she had a small pistol inside. How did she get a gun through customs? It was before today's strict laws."[1] I guess it was a memorable accessory.

On another occasion, André and I planned on going together to the Metropolitan Museum of Art's Costume Institute Gala (otherwise known as the "Met Ball"). It was in 2005, the year the museum celebrated the house of Chanel, and I wanted to wear a very special dress. André found one for me at LILY et Cie, the famous vintage boutique in Los Angeles. The store had a fabulous Chanel couture gown designed by Karl Lagerfeld for his second collection in 1984, and I bought it by telephone. Thankfully, the confection of black organza and lace fit. The night of the gala, André picked me up in a Maybach towncar and I could barely get the dress through the door. The skirt was so voluminous that it filled the back seat and blocked the rear window!

And let's not forget about the little *white* dress, especially in

---

1. André Leon Talley, *Little Black Dress* (New York: Rizzoli, 2013), 168.

the spring or summer, although now you can wear winter white in cashmere or in wool. I'm a big fan of shifts, probably a throwback to my Jackie Kennedy days, when that simple, beautifully cut swath of fabric seemed impossibly glamorous. Shifts flatter every figure and are very versatile, whether in summer white or winter black. Young girls don't have to worry about showing their arms (actually, young girls don't have to worry about much), but for those of us who want/need to cover them, I like to have a little wrap, maybe edged with fringe for a feminine touch.

For those moments when more is more, I like to pair a dress with a stunning coat. I fussed over what I should wear to the Bravos this year when I had the unusual distinction of being nominated for the Susan Lucci Award. Two of my conominees, Dorinda Medley and Vicki Gunvalson, are "Housewives," and the other, Kristen Doute, is on *Vanderpump Rules*. As Bravo fans know, these women are not afraid to be flashy. This was to

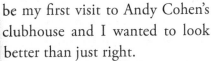

be my first visit to Andy Cohen's clubhouse and I wanted to look better than just right.

In the days leading up to the awards, I was torn between wearing white or black (should I be a good witch or a bad witch?). After much deliberation, I decided that white is more regal. The dress by Lanvin was lovely, but the coat was made of white silk and designed by The Row, and was a real showstopper, or should I say a "reality-showstopper." My outfit received rave reviews on social media and one admiring

On the red carpet at the Bravo Awards.

Southern Charm fan posted on Instagram that my "coat game is on another level."

I hadn't thought of coat wearing as an athletic event, but I will say that a beautiful evening coat is one of the smartest wardrobe investments you can make. A "duster" comes to the ground and has an even hem, while an "opera coat" is voluminous and has a train. You can pair an evening coat with anything from a slip to a gown, and if you're young, a minidress. If you dare, and your coat has a belt or buttons, you can be like Elizabeth Taylor in the film *Butterfield 8* and wear nothing at all under it. You can dress it up or down with accessories, and you'll find it will be the one garment you turn to season after season, year after year, when you want to look elegant.

Stockings or No Stockings?

There's controversy about whether or not to wear stockings—young girls can get by without wearing them, if the cold weather doesn't bother them. But I think that older women should wear them because they work miracles—they even out the skin tone, hold in what nature wants to spill out, and make legs and the lower torso look lean and shapely. If you ask me, SPANX stockings are the greatest invention of the twenty-first century.

When Did You Buy That Bra?

The right—or the wrong—bra can change everything. A personal stylist once told me that the worst mistake a woman can make is to wear a bra that doesn't fit properly. If you're in a store trying on clothes, ask if someone from the lingerie department can bring you a selection of bras to try on at the same time. Different garments require different foundations, and the only way to determine which bra fits best is through trial and error. Women appear years younger with proper uplift, so get frequent fittings and replace that old, loose bra that feels like a sling and makes you look saggy and baggy.

Caftans

I don't know how it happened, but I have become famous for my caftans. I'm the caftan queen. I have more caftans than Lawrence of Arabia. They are very chic and extremely comfortable—so comfortable that I see the caftan as an acceptable way to wear a nightgown in public.

People seem to think that I'm unique for swanning around in them, but I remember being inspired by photographs of great beauties wearing caftans in *Vogue* magazine in the 1960s. Fashion icons, including Talitha Getty, Marella Agnelli, and Elizabeth Taylor, posed in exotic locations, looking sun-kissed, romantic, and daring, their caftans blowing in the breeze. More recently, Kate Moss could be seen modeling a caftan in fashion layouts.

I first started wearing them in the 1970s, when they were still considered bohemian, and that was about as bohemian as I ever got. At the time, they were likely to be tie-dyed. Caftans were great for the beach and parties at home, and perfect if you were pregnant and trying to conceal a baby. Now, I have an entire wardrobe of caftans. They're so versatile that I wear them for many different kinds of occasions, and especially when I'm entertaining at home.

The trick is to select one that fits properly and to pair it with the right accessories. If you are tall, you can wear one that is voluminous because it will drape properly. If you are curvy or full-figured, a caftan offers great camouflage. And if you are petite, you want to make sure you get one that doesn't have an excessive amount of fabric. I like the ones that are stitched down the sides because they look loose and structured at the same time.

I've found my best caftans in a variety of places, from designer showrooms to a marketplace in India. At the moment, my favorite is a whimsical one designed by Libertine and called "Monkeys in Space," because the print is—guess what—monkeys in space. I love a caftan with a sense of humor.

Big, bold jewelry makes a caftan come to life. It is an exotic look and you should have fun with it. I do! Add cuffs, bracelets, heavy necklaces, dangly earrings, a multitude of rings, and you're good to go. Whether your jewelry is real or costume—and a mixture can be nice—a caftan is a great canvas for your most flamboyant, attention-getting pieces, and lots of them. Sometimes more is not enough.

You can add flat shoes or sandals for a casual effect. But when it is time to dress up, put on your highest heels and don't be shy. The wildest shoes I own are by Giuseppe Zanotti. They are black suede cages covered with turquoise, gemstones, and

Adventures in India.

spikes, and they have five-inch stiletto heels. I paired them with a white cashmere caftan and an Indian turquoise necklace. I couldn't walk in them—nobody can—but these amazing shoes turned a demure caftan into a sensation.

My passion for caftans has inspired me to start my own line with my friend and favorite entrepreneur, Georgette Mosbacher. It all started when we took a trip to India together and met Sherina Dalamal, a very successful young wedding dress designer. While we were there, we talked about how much we loved caftans and how it would be fun to have one with the image of a favorite pet on it. Georgette is obsessed with Guinevere, her Cavalier King Charles spaniel, and everyone knows how I feel about the members of my extended dog family. Sherina made a customized caftan for Georgette, and when everyone wanted it, we knew we were on to something.

Georgette and I have busy lives. When we travel together, we're girls who just want to have fun.

The last thing either of us needed was a business opportunity. But we couldn't resist the idea of

With Georgette Mosbacher, modeling our pet caftans from PatriciasCouture.com.

offering pet lovers a beautiful and lightweight caftan that can feature a silk-screened image of their dog or cat, or any animal (how about your pet iguana?). They're whimsical, comfortable, and extremely flattering. And I love the idea of draping myself in a fabric printed with Chauncey's sweet little face.

I've asked my friend Cathy Horyn, the fashion critic and journalist (who is working on a history of the fashion coverage in the *New York Times*, from the 1850s to the present), to share her thoughts on the enduring appeal of the caftan.

ASK THE EXPERT

Cathy Horyn

When did fashionable women start wearing caftans? What decade? Do you recall the first time you saw one in a fashion magazine, or on a celebrity?

I could imagine that the European heroines of Lesley Blanch's book *The Wilder Shores of Love* wore caftans or some variation while living in the Middle East, especially Jane Digby el Mezrab. We're talking about the mid-Victorian period. At the beginning of the twentieth century, the Paris couturier Paul Poiret created loose-fitting tunics and robes that were probably inspired by Arabic dress, including caftans. I remember seeing very vivid caftans in American *Vogue*, but primarily in issues from the 1960s and '70s—the Vreeland era. Oscar de la Renta always made them for his clients.

Is there any place you can't (or shouldn't) wear a caftan?

It's probably not a good idea to wear a caftan in church. Otherwise, depending on the color, fabric and embellishment, and how you accessorize your caftan, I think you can wear them anywhere. Caftans can also be short and belted. So, good for a more professional setting (though, again, depends on the type of work environment).

Caftans never seem to go out of style. What makes them timeless?

Caftans resist aging because, like Shaker furniture and the Chanel cardigan jacket, they have simple lines. They're sort of unanswerably chic, perhaps because of all those visual associations with wild Victorians, bohemians, and jet-setters of the past. Also, they're tasteful and practical, yet because they're loose in cut, they imply that the wearer is someone who doesn't like to be controlled.

What's the single most dramatic accessory a woman can pair with a caftan?

Because caftans are so simple, and a bit exotic, dramatic jewelry is the obvious accessory—something like the bronze-and-stone pieces that Lisa Eisner makes in Los Angeles.

Do you ever wear them?

My favorite caftan was one in lightweight gray wool from Yves Saint Laurent. Last year I had a pair of caftans—one black, one white, both short—made for me by the young designers of Monse, Laura Kim and Fernando Garcia. They're now the creative directors at Oscar de la Renta.

The Perfect Fit

I'm surprised more people don't know this: a good tailor can make a garment look as if it were made for you. Simple alterations—a slight pad to offset uneven shoulders, a hem adjustment, a seam taken in or let out—can make all the difference in the world. Bulges and pooches are never a good look, so buy the correct size and then let a tailor customize your clothing to minimize your flaws. I once read that Jennifer Aniston even has her T-shirts altered to fit perfectly.

Accessories and the Fur Flip

Shoes are my passion. Flats have their place in life, but can we talk about the magical powers of heels? They elongate the leg, sculpt pounds off the body, and give a woman stature, especially when she is beautifully dressed. Let the heels give you lift—stand up straight, shoulders back. Even if you are tall like me, don't be afraid to add height. But teetering is not a good look. Practice walking in your new heels so you don't look as if you are performing in Cirque du Soleil. If your stilettos are a little too high, take them to a good shoemaker. He can shorten them by almost an inch. You'll be more comfortable and no one will be the wiser.

Just as important as how you stand in heels is how you sit. Southern women are very good at sitting correctly, probably because our mothers were terrified we might expose the wrong thing at the wrong time. When I went to cotillion in Richmond, the ladies taught us to sit with our ankles crossed, but I think that position causes the legs to spread in an ungainly way. Here's a much more attractive way to sit: if you cross your legs at the knee, and keep your legs pressed together, foot pointing down, you will achieve an elegant, straight line. And try to sit up straight, shoulders open, without looking stiff. Slumping is diminishing. You want to present yourself properly, but you also want to look comfortable, and it can require a little practice to do both.

There's even a proper way to sit down when wearing a fur coat. I call it the "fur flip." Lift the hem of your coat and flip it up before you sit: you will literally break the fur if you put your weight on it.

On to my next favorite accessory: the purse. Have you noticed that purses have become much more important than their function? The philosophy seems to be: you are what you carry. I'm the first one to appreciate a gorgeous Hermès bag, or a classic Chanel, which are great investments, by the way, because they appreciate in value. I bought a bubble-gum-pink, one-of-a-kind, alligator Birkin bag strictly as an investment, because Birkin bags are bought and traded as commodities. I have never worn, nor carried it, anywhere. It sits pristine in its original box, waiting to be sold for a nice profit.

I think the big mistake most women make when selecting the right bag is to overlook the importance of scale. During the day, it is fine to carry the enormous satchel that holds everything you ever owned but can never find. However, if you haul that oversized bag to a cocktail party, you look as if you are coming to spend the night, which may not be the precise message you want to send. Evening bags should always be small—a little clutch, for example—holding lipstick, money, keys, and if you can squeeze it in, a cell phone. Just the essentials. My stylish friend Georgette Mosbacher puts her keys and her money in her shoe when she wants to be unencumbered. That's true freedom.

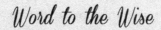

Word to the Wise

Never wait until the last minute to decide what you're going to wear, because that's the moment you will discover that something doesn't fit, doesn't look right with the ensemble, or needs to be repaired. Here's what I do, and it's failsafe. I assemble what I call my clothing **vignettes**. I decide what I'm going to wear—in this case an LBD—and lay everything out. My J. Mendel dress is fancy and has chiffon sleeves, so I pair it with sparkly Manolo Blahniks and a sequined Chanel purse. I'll decide what earrings I want to wear later on. But I usually take a picture, and I make a notation of where I'm going and what I'm wearing. It's a good way to keep a record and will prevent you from getting all flummoxed right before you go to a party because you've prepared in advance. You're much more relaxed, especially if you have that dressing drink.

> **Vignette:** a brief, but powerful, scene.

Tiaras

This question comes up more than you would think. When is it appropriate to wear a tiara? In my day, only married royals could wear a tiara. Judith Martin, otherwise known as "Miss Manners," suggests that tiaras are acceptable at the opera and when visiting with royalty, but never at brunch. Now, anything goes, especially with *Game of Thrones* being such a hit. You could wear one to the Piggly Wiggly and not feel out of place. Personally, I think it is inappropriate to wear a tiara unless you're going to a white-tie function. But if you insist on donning one for more **quotidian** events, you must wear it properly. Most people make the mistake of setting it too low on the forehead or too far back on the head. It should sit in the middle. I have a tiara that has a martini glass on it.

Quotidian: ordinary or everyday.

Jewelry

When I was growing up, one never wore diamonds in the daytime. That was considered déclassé and showy. My mother would have found some of the jewelry I wear enormously vulgar. But I enjoy shiny, pretty things and I don't hold back! Of course, if you have on jeans and a T-shirt, diamonds look silly (and don't get me started about that **oxymoron** the tennis bracelet. What diamonds and tennis have to do with each other I'll never know.) The diamond you can wear any time of day is an engagement ring, the bigger the better.

Oxymoron: a combination of words that have opposite or very different meanings.

If you are more conservative, pearls are always lovely and always appropriate. I think they add that polished Grace Kelly touch when you want to look demure. Wear them day or night, a choker at the neck or layered strands to the waist. I treasure my pink, opalescent South Sea pearls. But the best thing about pearls is that most people can't tell the difference between real and fake, so you don't have to be rich to enjoy them. My friend, the fabulous jewelry designer Kenneth Jay Lane, makes the most incredible faux pearls. No one could ever tell that they were fake, and every First Lady had a wardrobe of them.

Gloves

Pearls go hand in hand with gloves. I think gloves have fallen out of fashion because women don't know how to wear them anymore, which is a shame because gloves are elegant and sexy at the same time. I remember wearing evening gloves to an event and men couldn't stop kissing my hand. They were enthralled by the mystery of my covered flesh.

The rule of thumb for wearing gloves to a formal event is as follows:

- ◈ Gloves should always be made of classic white kid.
- ◈ Gloves should fit close to the skin—no wrinkles or bunching at the wrist.
- ◈ Above the elbow if you are wearing a full-length gown—up to the wrist or elbow (no higher), if you are wearing cocktail or semi-formal.
- ◈ Rings are worn underneath gloves.
- ◈ Bracelets are worn on top.
- ◈ Keep your gloves on to greet people and during cocktails.
- ◈ Remove gloves to eat and keep them in your lap—never put them on the table (this applies to purses, too).

The great thing about wearing gloves is that you don't need to use Purell after shaking hands with a lot of people!

Monograms and Family Crests

Like most Southerners, I'm a sucker for a monogram or a family crest. It goes back to the whole thing about genealogy and family, because as I said, all Southerners are really left with is their history. Monograms can be used just about anywhere—on stationery, on clothing and accessories, on linens, on china and silverware, and even on pet bowls. I saw a Rolls-Royce with both a monogram and a family crest and I kind of liked it.

Traditional monograms have the initial of the last name in the center, with the initials of the first and middle names on the left and right, respectively. In my day, married women used their initials on their sheets, towels, and table linens. But today, monograms are the Wild West: there are templates for couples, singles, people with hyphenated last names, and every other combination. I prefer the old-fashioned way, but if you want to be unconventional, there are internet resources to help you figure it out.

If you don't know your family crest, you can research it. Many names have European roots that go all the way back to medieval times, when families used coats of arms and crests. Trace your family history at **Ancestry.com** or hire a genealogist to do it for you. You can also start the tradition for yourself and future generations by using an online tool (there's actually a site called **FamilyCrest.com**) to assemble the various symbols that make up a crest. If all else fails, there are artists who will do it for you.

You can put a family crest anywhere. I have it on towels, linens, stationery—and Whitney has our family crest tattooed on his arm. I'd love it if it weren't so big.

Decoding the Dress Code

We live in a casual world, is the polite way of putting it, where the bar is set very low. When I was growing up in the fifties, women knew how to dress up. In fact, they wore dresses and high heels, their hair was done, and their makeup was in place on a Tuesday morning, when they had no plans. They were party-ready *all the time*. There are times when you have to take off your exercise clothes, put on the dog, and be as glamorous as you can, especially for parties. That said, you don't want to make a mistake because you misunderstood the dress code.

Oscar Wilde once said that you can never be overdressed or overeducated, but I disagree about the overdressed part. You don't want to be the one who sticks out like a sore thumb at a party, and invitations can be very confusing, especially when a host uses the dress code to elevate the event. How else do you explain a "black-tie pig roast at the beach," and how do you figure out what to wear to it? I always analyze the occasion and the location—*pig roast* and *beach*

Is a Speedo ever in fashion?

Shep and Whitney—I love a man who knows how to dress for a Flamingo party!

tell you everything you need to know. You should not be dressing formally for this party. In fact, you probably shouldn't go!

"Black tie" is a pretty straight-forward directive for men: it means wear a tuxedo. But for women, "black tie" is a broad category that breaks down in the following ways:

Cameran, Whitney, and Landon—dressed to kill.

- ◈ Gowns are reserved for really formal occasions, such as a ball.
- ◈ Weddings and other events call for a cocktail-length dress.
- ◈ If a party is in a tent, or on the grass, wear wedge heels.

In my experience, parties with dress codes tend to be long, so think about comfort.

One of the most confusing dress codes on an invitation is "black tie optional." I don't like anything that's optional because it opens the door to some guests dressing in their finest while others show up in cowboy boots and sombreros. If you're the host, be specific, or your event will be a mashup of the prom and the office Christmas party. If you really don't care what people wear, tell them up front. Just say "party attire," or "festive attire," and let them go wild.

These days, very few events are "white tie." The Met Ball comes to mind. If it comes up, women should wear long, formal evening gowns (and you can dust off that tiara). Men have an

THE ART OF SOUTHERN CHARM

elaborate list of wardrobe requirements, including a white bow tie, a waistcoat, and patent leather shoes.

British Vogue offers a useful way to determine what an invitation is really saying when it comes to dress code. "The thicker the card (and the more fanciful the calligraphy); the smarter the event. If it came via Facebook, you can relax a little," the magazine suggests.

Maintaining Your Wardrobe

The *New York Times* says that well-kept clothes signify adulthood.[2] What is the point of collecting beautiful garments if you don't take care of them? I mentioned that it is a good idea to inspect your outfits and accessories well before you need to wear them so that repairs can be made. An even better idea is to examine your clothes immediately after your wear them, before you put them away. Marie Kondo, author of the best-selling book *The Life-Changing Magic of Tidying Up*, would agree. Check for stains, loose buttons, and droopy hems—problems don't fix themselves while the clothes are hanging in the closet, as nice as that would be. In fact, they usually get worse.

My English friends have a unique and highly effective way of maintaining their wardrobes. They don't believe in sending clothes to the dry cleaner unless it is absolutely necessary. Instead, they hang their clothes in special airing rooms, spot-clean them, and use the appropriate brushes to remove surface dust and dirt. Obviously, if you spill red wine on your white coat you need a professional. But most of the time an airing and

2. Vanessa Friedman, "How to Dress Like an Adult," *New York Times*, October 26, 2016.

a vigorous brushing will do the trick. Chemicals are not good for fine garments, but you can use an organic dry cleaner, if you can find one.

I hand wash my cashmere sweaters and lay them out on a mesh platform to dry, instead of draping them on the balcony so it looks like Naples. Here's a tip I'm happy to pass on: use products by The Laundress for your fine washables. A friend and I were remarking that their delicate soaps, fabric sprays, and tools (all beautifully packaged) actually make doing laundry fun. And the scent is really clean. I'm all for bringing back clotheslines, so everything can be dried in the sun.

My big indulgence is that I like to have everything freshly ironed, even my nightgowns. When I was growing up, my mother taught me the best way to iron anything. For example, a blouse:

◈ Wash and air dry, then sprinkle with distilled water.
◈ Roll the damp blouse and place it in the refrigerator overnight.
◈ Iron the next day.

My laundry room has a mangle, an old-fashioned device used to press sheets, towels, and napkins. Lucky me, having someone to do all that. But I have a young friend, a newlywed, in fact, who shares my mania for pressed surfaces and neat creases and she does it all herself. She even irons the sheets before she puts them on the bed.

I live in an historic home, so I do not have a Carrie Bradshaw, *Sex and the City*–style oversized closet. What I've done to compensate is create two separate closets, one for my casual clothes and shoes and one for my cocktail dresses, suits, and heels. I've given most of my ballgowns away because I no longer live in

New York, so my lifestyle has changed, but I keep the remaining ones in a cedar closet.

An old-fashioned cedar closet, a popular and effective way of preventing moths since the seventeenth century, is a great addition to any home. It's not that difficult (or expensive) to convert a regular closet into one that protects your out-of-season clothes from pests and mildew. If you are at all handy, you can purchase cedar planks from Home Depot or a lumber store, and fit them to the walls, ceiling, and floor of an existing closet with adhesive and nails. Or, you can hire a carpenter or a handyman to do it. Your clothes will last longer and smell fresh and natural, like a forest.

The caftans—well, that's another story. They're multiplying on a rack and taking over entire rooms when I'm not looking. However you organize your closet, never hang knits—they lose their shape. And if you use a dry cleaner, always remove the clothing from the plastic and air it out before putting away. A garment bag should be made out of a material that breathes, such as cotton.

Traveling in Style

I love to travel and I do it often. Whether I'm going to New York, Los Angeles, or Europe, my travel routine is always the same, and it has served me well. When I'm planning what to pack, I try to restrict myself to a black-and-white wardrobe because it's easier to create multiple looks from a highly curated selection of clothing and use the same accessories—usually black flats and heels. I rely on an assortment of scarves to add color.

Never, ever, use fancy luggage—it invites trouble. You

might as well tell thieves to shop *here*. You want your bags to be plain and utilitarian, not an advertisement for the fabulous things you've packed, so to keep thieves at bay, restrict logos to items *inside* the bag. I've just purchased gold Raden luggage, which in addition to being strong and utilitarian, has a built-in phone charger and an app that enables you to track your bag. Once you have the perfect suitcase, attach a bright, colorful luggage tag so you can identify it when all the other nondescript bags come pouring onto the carousel.

The only time I break my rule about luggage is when I pack my cosmetics. I have an old-fashioned Louis Vuitton train case that is so old and beat-up that I hesitate to use the word *vintage* to describe it. The strap is broken and the leather is worn, but it is the perfect size and shape to accommodate all the bottles and tubes I need on a trip. I fill it with makeup, creams, nail products, eye drops, brushes, *anything* that might come up—and I check it with my luggage.

The same people who spend hours on wardrobe choices at home never give a thought to how they look when they travel. Dress comfortably, but with style. I wear monochromatic cashmere pants and a sweater, an elegant, understated combination that is comfortable and can hold up on long flights. If cashmere is not a part of your wardrobe, wear something soft—leggings and a top—and keep the color palette neutral. Some of the new, well-cut athleta-wear (not baggy sweats!) can serve the same purpose. For footwear, I recommend flat shoes. A ballerina flat is perfect—easy to walk in and easy to remove at security.

What you carry onto the plane can be as important as what you wear. I always have a roomy tote large enough to accommodate my medicine, an eye mask, a pashmina that can double as a blanket (airplanes are always cold), a baby pillow, magazines, my iPad, and antibacterial wipes. I also carry my jewelry, which I keep in a Louis Vuitton case (never make the mistake of packing valuables in your suitcase). I try not to take super-expensive jewels on a trip—better to pack less flashy, or costume, pieces. I like cuffs, bangles, and necklaces by Ashley Pittman. The jewelry, which is stunning, is made by artisans in Kenya, who are employed and given business development training by the company.

As soon as I'm in my seat I use a wipe to clean the armrest, tray, and seatbelt, so I look like I'm part of the cleaning crew. And by the way, never put anything in the seat pocket—who knows what's been living in there since the previous flight. Someone once told me that it has more germs than any other part of the airplane.

Let's Behave

I'M NOT A **PERSNICKETY** PERSON, BUT I DO BELIEVE that good manners improve the quality of life for everyone. The word *manners* is defined as "the way that a person normally behaves, especially while with other people." I like this definition because it suggests that we should be on our best behavior every day. My parents gave me a classic Southern upbringing that began with "please" and "thank you," and "yes, ma'am," and "no, sir." As I got older, my social education continued. My world expanded and I learned the proper way to behave in it. Some people think these concerns are frivolous, but all of this "frivolity" is important to me because it makes life beautiful and so much more enjoyable.

Persnickety: placing too much emphasis on trivial or minor details, fussy.

Let's review a few of the basics:

◈ Always say please and thank you. Do I really have

to remind you? Treat everyone with equal respect. I think it is always very telling of character when someone behaves beautifully with their peers, but is a monster to servicepeople.

◈ Cell phone addiction is the new smoking and my list of "don'ts" is long (and growing): no cell phones at the table; no loud, personal conversations in public; and stop going to the restroom to check your Instagram—we know what you're doing!

◈ Do not chew gum, ever.

◈ Never be late without a very good excuse.

◈ Always respond to an invitation promptly. If you can't attend, follow Arthur's example. He always said, "I'm sorry, I have a conflict." You don't have to explain because no one ever asks what that conflict is.

These everyday rules are pretty straightforward and will serve you well at home and in the world. Some social situations can be trickier to navigate, and I'm going to help you get through them with **panache**.

What happens when you enter a gathering? Do you hesitate and wait for someone to approach you? Do you position yourself on the sidelines, desperately hoping to spot a familiar face?

Panache: flamboyant confidence of style or manner.

There is only one proper way to introduce yourself in any social situation, whether you are walking into a finished basement or a ballroom. Move purposefully, extend your hand, and say with the greatest confidence, "How do you do? I'm (your name)." The person will respond with a handshake and his/her name, and inevitably, pleasantries will follow. Continue the conversation as long as it is interesting, until you politely move on to introduce yourself to others.

For those moments when you stare at someone, knowing you've met before, but are drawing a complete blank, try this ingenious tip. Say, "Remind me of your name," and when they tell you their first name, answer, "No, not your first name, I know that" (as if you knew it all along), "your *last* name."

If you are making introductions, say the older person's name first: "Father Time, I'd like you to meet Baby New Year." But if there's a woman involved, she comes first, as in "Cleopatra, I'd like you to meet Julius Caesar." That is, unless you are introducing her to the president of the United States. In that case, he or she comes before anyone else.

Word to the Wise

Never ask someone what he or she does for a living. That is not the Southern way. A more indirect—and infinitely more genteel—approach is to say, "Tell me about yourself," which gives the person the opportunity to take the conversation in many different directions, and to write their own narrative. They can talk about their interests, their family, and anything else that comes to mind. Better still, you avoid embarrassing someone who does not have a job.

I love dinner parties, but I know that members of the takeout generation can be intimidated by the sight of a formally set table, with its minefield of silverware, plates, and glasses. It's actually easy to figure out. When you sit down, unfold your napkin and place it on your lap. The place setting in front of you is organized in a logical way according to the order in which the implements will be used, working from the outside inward toward the plate. For example, on the left side of the plate, the salad fork is to the left of the dinner fork because it is used before the dinner fork, because salad is served before the main course. On the extreme right, glasses also line up according to their function, beginning with the water glass and proceeding to the wine glasses.

I just came across a funny way to help you distinguish your bread plate area and your glass area from your neighbor's turf. Place your hands (discreetly) on the table and make an "OK" sign with both index fingers and thumbs. The left hand will look like the letter "b," for *bread*, while the right hand will look like the letter "d," for *drink*. Simple!

If you're still confused about what to use when, watch your host for cues. Wait for your host to pick up her/his fork before you start eating. And, as I'm sure your mother told you, never, ever, speak with your mouth full.

Here Are a Few of My Favorite Things...

- Cashmere scarves and embroidered purses from India
- SPANX
- Lip balm by Fresh (I'm addicted to that)
- Candy corn
- Clinique Non-Oily Eye Make-Up Remover
- Dogs, all varieties and lots of them
- Cats, all varieties and lots of them
- Horses, all varieties and lots of them

- Blue-and-white porcelain, whether it is from William-Wayne, one of my favorite stores for all things chic in NYC (and online at **william-wayne.com**), Pier 1, or Christie's. If you like it, buy it!
- Alkaline water from Whole Foods (it counteracts inflammation)
- Box of sharpened decorative pencils and a matching holder filled with notepaper from Il Papiro, NYC—I have them all over the house
- Needlepoint—you can buy it from antique stores or, if you're talented like my mother, make it yourself
- Clarisonic Mia2 for face cleaning
- Claus Porto Madrigal water lily soap
- Decorative pineapples, monkeys, elephants…
- Léron quilted bed jacket
- Powder puffs, because they're pretty and feminine
- Shoes with pom-poms

A beautiful day with my beautiful Lily.

And My Least Favorite Things...

Alice Roosevelt Longworth, daughter of Theodore Roosevelt, is credited with saying, "If you don't have anything nice to say, come sit next to me." In that spirit, I've listed what we used to call "pet peeves." I don't have anything nice to say about...

- ◈ Toilet paper folded into points—and worse than that, toilet paper folded and topped with a sticker
- ◈ Fake Christmas trees
- ◈ Cheap chocolate
- ◈ Cheap potpourri
- ◈ Man buns
- ◈ Carnations and gladiola
- ◈ Calling curtains "drapes"
- ◈ Fruit arrangements—I don't want fruit if it's in a box and I don't know who touched it
- ◈ Bringing untrained puppies to visit
- ◈ People who don't watch TCM (Turner Classic Movies)
- ◈ French manicures
- ◈ Women or men who wear too much cologne
- ◈ Ugly shoes on women (the overly masculine ones— you know what I mean)
- ◈ Side boob
- ◈ Brushing hair in public
- ◈ Chewing gum
- ◈ Green or blue fingernail polish
- ◈ Checking lipstick on a knife—for God's sake, get up and go to the restroom!
- ◈ Talking about how much something costs
- ◈ Miniskirts on older women

And Then There's the End of Western Civilization...

- ◈ Visible piercings
- ◈ Underwear that's worn in place of real clothing in public
- ◈ Flip-flops, except at the beach
- ◈ Talking about fibroids, prostates, or sperm counts at the table

Smart is the New Sexy

WE'RE ALL FAMILIAR WITH THE LIFE LESSONS BEHIND *EAT, PRAY, Love*, Elizabeth Gilbert's wonderful book about how to find and experience your passion. Well, I'm going to do my version of the sequel, and I'm calling it *Speak, Write, Read.* I'm a woman who thinks that smart is the new sexy. I believe in Southern belles, not dumb belles, wherever they're from. With time, effort, and practice you can polish your social skills to perfection and move gracefully through all situations.

How You Speak Says it All

Have you ever been in a restaurant and thought about throttling the man or the woman you can hear even when they're on the other side of the room? When their sounds intrude on your space, something is wrong. My mother and the nuns at school were militant about teaching me the proper way to speak. First and foremost, I learned to modulate my voice to make it soft and pleasing to the ear. I remember my mother saying, "Keep it down, I can hear you." If there is no mother (or nun) there to correct you, you'll have to do it yourself.

Pay attention to how you sound in a group. Are you louder than everyone else? Is your voice harsh? Do you speak too fast? I think Southerners are great **raconteurs**, with rich, melodious voices that are enhanced, of course, by the drawl. I'm not advocating appropriating the drawl—that's a Southern privilege—but you can certainly slow down the pace.

> **Raconteur:** a person who tells anecdotes in a skillful and amusing way.

Always choose your words carefully. When it comes to speech, I'm ready for a cultural revolution. Why does everyday language have to be so foul? Today, grannies and children alike use expletives that would have sent my mother running to her bed. In our house, being "common" was the worst crime you could commit, and using coarse language was definitely considered common.

Some adults pepper their speech with curses and slang because they want to appear younger or hip, but I think modern **vernacular** is really slippage. I don't like abbreviations—words like "adorbs," "gorg," and "vacay." And "yo, dude" and "whassup" send me into the stratosphere. I believe that speech should be authentic, and I'm never afraid to be perceived as proper. You can still have fun in life if you occupy a higher plane. And can we put an end to all of these direct references to body parts? I wish we'd go back to the days when we said "down there," if you know what I mean.

> **Vernacular:** the language or dialect spoken by the ordinary people in a particular country or region.

So here's my challenge to anyone who wants to improve the way they sound. Try to get through an hour, a day, a week, without using a four-letter word as your default response. There's always another way to express yourself, and I guarantee that you will not be considered odd or square (if that's even a word anymore).

Since we're no longer swearing to express disapproval, let's discuss that fabulous, all-purpose, and extremely useful Southern staple, the stealth insult. Southerners, and especially Southern women, may be famous for their honeybee charm and hospitality, but don't be fooled. Southerners aren't all sugar: there's plenty of spice in what they say. I am known for my candor, and one of the best compliments I ever received, in a tweet no less, was "@pataltschul is so elegant that even when she insults you, you kinda feel like it was a compliment." A well-phrased insult can still have a charm all its own.

As they live and breathe, Southerners have elevated the insult to an art form. Nobody does it better. "You don't say," which seems to indicate surprise or delight, usually means "how boring," or "boy, I've heard that before!" Every **faux** compliment is followed by an invisible thought bubble that says something completely different.

Faux: not genuine, fake or false.

My favorite is "Bless your heart" or "Bless his/her heart." This seemingly innocent statement has a myriad of negative connotations and is usually more of a condemnation than a blessing. I say it all the time. "Look at Betsy, bless her heart." (Her dress is hideous.) "Did you see what Frank did, bless his heart?" (How stupid is he?)

Other classic, under-the-radar insults include:

◈ "Aren't you sweet?" when a person is the opposite.
This is how I generally respond to nasty internet trolls.

◈ "Isn't that something…" *That's the ugliest baby I've ever seen.*

◈ "I couldn't pull that look off, but look at you…" *Actually, you look terrible.*

It's all about the delivery. Southerners know that you really can say *anything* if you smile and speak in a pleasant tone. A direct hit in a velvet glove.

Finally, when you're talking to someone, don't be afraid to be quiet. I always admire people who are comfortable with short silences in a conversation. The less secure person rushes in to fill the void, chattering twice as fast. But that's just a nervous tic. Pause. Be still. Be circumspect. Never interrupt or monopolize a conversation. As mother would say, "think before you speak."

Getting it Write

The most successful people I know have mastered the art of writing a note. It is an age-old method of communication that never goes out of style. The process—thought to pen, pen to paper, paper to person—creates a tangible connection between the writer and the recipient. Your penmanship, regardless of what it looks like, expresses your personality. Your carefully chosen words convey your sentiments. Emails and texts have their place in life, but the written word makes a deeper impression than a fleeting message that probably has more emojis than characters.

Admittedly it is not as easy as it sounds to dash off a note of thanks, condolence, congratulations, or even a casual "thinking of you." If you have to scramble for the stationery, the pen, the stamp, the snail mail address, and then find the words, you probably won't do it. Being prepared can help you to be a more efficient communicator. Here's what you need to have in place:

An Up-to-date Contact List

I'm a little old and new school when it comes to maintaining addresses—I have a classic leather book, with detailed A to Z listings, and an extensive computer index that gets updated frequently.

I understand that this is where the smartphone can be really smart. Text or email your friends for their contact information and save it in your phone. You can also take advantage of the other fields to add birthdays, social handles, the name of that spouse, child, or assistant you can never remember, and notes about everything from dietary preferences to phobias. If you keep it up, you will have full profiles of your friends and business associates at your fingertips.

I should tell you that I have help with this, and all the other perplexing administrative details in my life, from my personal assistant of fourteen years, Joan DiPietro. Joan is indispensable because she is accomplished in so many areas. I depend on her for everything from scheduling, bill paying, tax preparation, spreadsheets, and curatorial work, to anything else that comes up.

A Stationery Wardrobe

That's right, a wardrobe. To write a proper note, you need proper stationery—in fact, you need a selection, ranging from formal to informal. People have gotten out of the habit of ordering personalized stationery, but there are so many resources, at all different price points. I always get my stationery from Mrs. John L. Strong, and I order both cards and sheets, with matching envelopes. I have cream-colored cards embossed with my family crest; letter sheets with a cutout monogram and a border; everyday cards with a green monogram; and foldover notes that say *Mrs. Arthur Altschul* on the front. If you must choose one all-purpose piece of stationery, a monogrammed card is the most versatile. The point is to have supplies available when you need them.

Your stationery can display your name, your name and address, your monogram, or some combination. If you're ordering online, there are tools to help you design the look you want. Experiment with different fonts, colors, and shapes. You can also select the weight of the paper, the method of printing, and whether or not your envelopes have liners. If you want people to have your email address, add it to your information.

Sometimes the biggest obstacle to mailing a note is not having a stamp. Solve that problem by buying forever stamps, aptly named because it will take you forever to finish the roll, and the postage is always good. A nice touch is to order customized stamps with a photograph of your home, or another image that is meaningful to you.

Put some thought into what kind of pens you enjoy using. I know it sounds silly, but words seem to flow better with the right pen. I recently discovered that there are disposable fountain pens that make the worst handwriting look elegant. They're not expensive and they can be ordered from any online office store. Some people like Flair pens with whimsically colored ink. I'm a traditionalist; I use a Chopard pen. When I'm out of the house, I always use my own pen when I sign a receipt because a million people have touched the pen they hand to you. Once you've assembled your supplies, keep them together in an attractive box or a drawer, and pull them out the moment you have the impulse—or the obligation—to write to someone.

You may think that finding the right words is the hardest part of composing a note. While I have a certain style—and I will share it with you—I find that the best sentiments are those that are immediate and from the heart. Babe Paley, Truman Capote's chief swan and one of modern society's greatest arbitresses of good taste, had an ironclad rule: she wrote (and sent) her thank-you notes while she still felt thankful, which meant as soon as she received a gift, or came home from being entertained. I'm not always that efficient, but I try to attend to it while the details are still fresh in my mind.

Let's say I have just been to my friend Carolyne Roehm's for dinner. She's so creative that the table is always a memorable

Word to the Wise

The one time you do not have to write a thank-you note is if someone gives you a hostess gift. Thank them profusely at the time. And guests take note: handing a bouquet to a hostess is what the French call a "poison gift." The last thing she needs is to have to find a vase and arrange flowers at the very moment she should be attending to her guests. It is much more considerate to present a beautifully potted orchid, or to have flowers delivered the next day. Or, you can give her this book!

part of the meal. That night or the very next day, I sit at my desk, select the appropriate piece of stationery, and recall the evening. I tell her how much I enjoyed dining in front of the fireplace, or how the colorful flowers made me think of spring. I try to remember how I felt at the moment (which is easier if it just happened), and that's what I write about.

Condolences can be hard to express. When thinking of what to say to a friend who has lost a loved one, consider what *you* would like to hear. If you knew the person, even in passing, try to recall an anecdote—small details mean so much. I once wrote to a bereaved friend recalling a conversation I'd had with her late husband, when we had a lively difference of opinion. My friend didn't know the story and was so happy to hear it. If someone I know has lost a parent, I remind them that they were a wonderful daughter or son.

If you did not know the deceased, offer words that are simple and sincere. "I'll keep you in my thoughts," or "in my prayers," if you're religious. The act of acknowledging someone's loss is a meaningful message in itself.

When the occasion is happy, and you're sending congratulations, you probably know exactly what to say: "How wonderful!" "I'm so happy!" "Enjoy your success/the baby/your marriage!" Genuine enthusiasm (and exclamation points) will do all the work for you. For this kind of note, feel free to use your less formal, more whimsical stationery. Some shops sell beautiful vintage cards, or you can collect attractive postcards from art museum gift shops.

Reading is More Fun than Sex

Well, that got your attention! I'm exaggerating, just a little. Reading makes us smarter. But it is also important for mental health as well as for social skills. I read five newspapers a day: the *New York Times*, the *New York Post*, the *Wall Street Journal*, the *Financial Times*, and the *Post-Courier*. I don't read everything in all of them, but by the time I finish, I feel well informed. I even read the *National Enquirer* because I think that pop culture says a lot about our country and our values. Andy Warhol loved the *Enquirer*, and I can see why. In addition to newspapers, I read all kinds of magazines and books—from bestsellers to classics.

Word to the Wise

I've expanded my vocabulary by reading. Many of the words I use come from nineteenth-century fiction and are slightly archaic. *Strumpet*, for example, which can be found in the works of Shakespeare, is much more eloquent than *skank* or *ho*. And *pedestrian* and **banal** sound better than just calling something boring. You will find great words in classics by Henry James, Jane Austen, Charles Dickens, Anthony Trollope, and Colette, to name a few. And if you don't know what they mean, check a dictionary or type them into Google and look them up!

Banal: so lacking in originality as to be obvious and boring.

What's in My Kindle?

Anyone peeking into my Kindle would be amused by the range of books that appeal to me. Fiction, nonfiction, great literature, guilty pleasures…I am always reading several books simultaneously. Lately I've enjoyed:

- ◈ *Belgravia*, by Julian Fellowes, the creator of *Downton Abbey*. I also loved his novel *Snobs*.
- ◈ *Crazy Rich Asians* and *China Rich Girlfriend* by Kevin Kwan. Can't wait for the next book in the trilogy.
- ◈ *The Knockoff* by my friend Lucy Sykes
- ◈ *The Swans of Fifth Avenue* by Melanie Benjamin
- ◈ *Bright, Precious Days* by Jay McInerney
- ◈ *Gertrude Bell, Queen of the Desert, Shaper of Nations* by Georgina Howell
- ◈ *Under the Tuscan Sun* by Frances Mayes
- ◈ *The Andy Cohen Diaries: A Deep Look at a Shallow Year* and *Superficial* by the one and only Andy Cohen
- ◈ *Beach Music* by Pat Conroy
- ◈ *Midnight in the Garden of Good and Evil* by John Berendt
- ◈ *Party of the Century: The Fabulous Story of Truman Capote and His Black and White Ball* by Deborah Davis

As much as I like reading on my iPad, I have the greatest respect and appreciation for physical books and have collected them my entire life. I have a formal library with ceiling-to-floor books, bookcases in other parts of the house, and freestanding stacks everywhere. I'm always surprised when I walk into a home that doesn't have leaning towers of books—they reveal so much about a person. One glance at my books would tell you that I am fascinated by art and Southern history, that I love to entertain, and that I have a sense of humor (I have a book called *Dog Parties: Entertaining Your Party Animals*).

Like, Love, Marriage . . .
and Everything in Between

You're healthy, confident, you have a great sense of personal style, you know how to dress, and you have impeccable manners. Why, then, is it so hard to find a mate? I am asked this question all the time, and by the most appealing people of all ages. First of all, have you noticed that there's no mystery or romance in the world anymore? Women make themselves so available. You can text a woman an emoji of a glass of wine, and she'll come over, you have sex, and she goes home. It's the end of Western civilization as far as I can tell. I certainly wouldn't call that a *relationship*. I don't even like to use the term *one-night stand*. I prefer to say "Southern sleepover." There's a very different playbook for people who are interested in having relationships that might last longer than one night. The question is how—and where—do you find a man or a woman who is a keeper?

The night I met Lon, my first husband, we were at a large party in Washington. I remember it vividly. We were introduced by a mutual friend, we were both intrigued by each other, and, being Southern, I managed to project just the right air of availability and reserve. Lon was with a date, but the moment she went to the ladies' room, he asked for my telephone number. Sure enough, he followed up with a call. I sensibly reached out to other friends who knew him before I agreed to go out on a date, but destiny had spoken. That chance introduction led to marriage.

Actually, a friend introduced me to my second husband, too. Call me old-fashioned, but at a time when everyone is saying "OkCupid," I think the best way to meet a potential boyfriend or girlfriend is through mutual friends. People are afraid to ask, but there's no shame in announcing you're open to meeting someone and you'd like help. If they can think of a prospect, all they have to do is reach out to him or her and say, "I want you to call this person. I think you would enjoy their company."

When possibilities arise, be adventurous and go out for drinks and dinners. I don't believe there is just one person in the world for you. Chances are you will be kissing a lot of frogs (metaphorically) before you find your prince. There will be good nights and bad nights. If that exploratory date is not right, don't waste time: move on.

A friend of mine experienced a terrible **gaffe** while on a blind date. At the end of the evening, the man suggested that they play the childhood game rock, paper, scissors—essentially, an extended coin toss—for the check. She lost, and he handed her the bill and went off into the night. I wonder if all his dates end in a free meal?

Gaffe: a mistake made in a social situation.

Here's my personal checklist of what makes a first date a last date. Dump any man (or woman) who...

◈ Has inappropriate piercings and is sloppily dressed (that rules out half of the population). Remember, how a person dresses says something about whether or not they care about the date.

◈ Displays side boob (ladies, that's you).

◈ Greets you with a canned or cheesy opening.

◈ Is self-absorbed and talks only about himself all night.

◈ Has no sense of humor.

◈ Speaks badly about his parents (that's a big red flag).

And this may be a Southern thing, but I'm instantly turned off when a man doesn't stand up when you enter the room, or hold your chair when you sit.

Word to the Wise

I'm going to raise **hackles** here, but I believe that a real gentleman picks up his date and escorts her home at the end of the evening. Of course, women are capable of transporting themselves, and sometimes logic (or geography) dictates that they will do so—for example, if you are meeting a man for the first time and want to keep your address private until you know him a little better. But a man who offers to call for his date and see to it that she gets home safely, even in an Uber, demonstrates interest, consideration, and fine manners.

Hackles: erectile hairs along the back of a dog or other animal that rise when it is angry or alarmed.

There are times when both people do everything right and are on their very best behavior, yet there is absolutely no chemistry between them. You know when you are genuinely attracted to someone and feel a connection. I believe in the power of pheromones. We euphemistically refer to sex as the "birds and the bees" for a reason: nature is in control, dictating our emotions. When you don't feel that spark, always be gracious and kind, but you don't have to agree to a second date. Finding the best partner is not an easy job. It took me three times to get it right. Fortunately, we live in an age of recycling. If at first you don't succeed…

And here's my formula for a winning first date. The problem with young women today is that they don't know how to be closers—this is how you should behave if you want a date to go well, and it can work for both men and women, actually. You're not too enthusiastic. You're pleasant, but you don't come on too strong because it can be off-putting. Whitney thinks it's wrong to play games—he's all for instant "honesty." But with my many years of experience, I've learned some things. You have to get to know people in stages. If you know too much of them right away, all the mystery is gone. Not only that, much of what people divulge shouldn't be revealed in the first place. There are certain things that you should keep secret. I believe that!

This **caveat** also applies to how much skin you reveal. I think women should wear something demure on a first date. Keep the **décolletage** to a minimum. You don't want a lot of bosom showing, and you don't want to wear a miniskirt. Instead, pair something ladylike with high heels. I'm telling my age, but I would wear a simple, beautifully cut dress with pearls. I

Caveat:
a warning or proviso of specific stipulations, conditions, or limitations.

Décolletage:
a woman's cleavage as revealed by a low neckline.

would try to avoid looking like you-know-who, the Whore of Babylon. I asked Carson Kressley, the charming fashion expert, television personality, and author of the new book *Does This Book Make My Butt Look Big?*, for his thoughts on what to wear when you want to impress a date.

ASK THE EXPERT

Carson Kressley

First dates can be terrifying for a number of reasons. Thankfully, we can turn to Carson Kressley, the Emmy-winning television star and the author of *Does This Book Make My Butt Look Big?* (among other titles), for the answer to the all-important question both women and men want to ask…

Getting cozy with Carson Kressley.

WHAT DO I WEAR?

We have all heard the phrase "dress for success" and Southern women know wearing the right thing at the right time is crucial! Dressing for a date is like dressing for any other event (wedding, job interview, debutante ball) and it should be treated with equal deference! What you wear could change the course of your future forever! One of my favorite quotes from my hero Tom Ford, and I have many, is "dressing well is a form of good manners." Keep that in mind when dressing for a date. How you present yourself really tells the other person how much you care about and value them. If you are dating someone you really like, it's worth the effort and just plain good Southern manners to present yourself well. You'll feel better about yourself too, which ups your confidence level—which is very attractive!

What kind of an image should I project? Truth, fiction, or fantasy?

Clothes have the power to convey all three, so I think it should be a combination of all three! You should project the best possible version of you! If you are a jeans-and-T-shirt kind of gal, why not up the ante a bit and wear dark jeans and a super pretty and feminine top with great shoes and accessories? That way you will be comfortable in a wardrobe that's very much "you" but amped up for the location.

Is there a formula (in a good way), for the perfect outfit? What do you recommend?

First of all, make sure the clothes are well tailored, clean, and something you are comfortable in. Here's an easy formula— have the main garment be something you're comfortable and confident in—not sloppy, though! (This could be a great pair of jeans or a flirty skirt or a sexy dress.) Then add one element that is sexy or flirty. It could be a lacy bra, a pouty red lip, or a sexy heel. Pretty with a cool edge is what you are going for.

Oh, and one last thing: all Southern women know that "only whores and children wear red shoes." I promise you I did not make this up. Southern legend at its best, and great advice I think.

I'm coming right from work—how can I transition my look from daytime to DATE?

This one's easy. It's all about accessories. Simply change the shoes, bag, and earrings! Go from flats to heels or a strappy sandal. Switch out your big "day" bag to a sparkly clutch. Then pop on a statement earring and you're ready for some rosé and Prince Charming!

Now that you know how to dress properly, what's the best destination? Go out for cocktails for that first look. I wouldn't commit to anything beyond that right off the bat. Here are some other tips:

- ◈ Pick a romantic place, like the Bemelmans Bar, if you are in New York City. It's dark and atmospheric and you can't really hear yourself talk there, which might be good.
- ◈ Food first. Don't drink on an empty stomach. You don't want to get **snockered** at the outset.
- ◈ No hard liquor. Order a glass of rosé, or a beer, if the date is really casual.
- ◈ Or maybe don't drink at all. You don't want to watch him sip a Diet Coke while you slug down a giant-size Sex on the Beach.

Snockered: drunk.

◈ Have a sense of humor: no one wants to hear about your issues, your exes, or your breakups.

◈ Keep the first date to an hour. You want to leave people hungry for more of your company, and they can't feel that way if you don't leave!

So you made it through cocktails and you're looking forward to your second encounter—probably a proper dinner date. Again, dress appropriately. And, as you sit at the table, contemplating your menu, remember that *how* you order is very important the first time you share a meal. Your date doesn't want to listen to a diva reciting a high-maintenance list of foods she cannot eat, like, "I don't eat gluten. I don't eat salt. I don't eat meat. I'm on the Paleo diet." Keep your food rules to yourself. All your "don'ts" are boring, and if all goes well, you will have plenty of time to reveal your idiosyncrasies later.

Whitney told me about a funny experience he had on a dinner date. He was out with a model who ordered two California rolls. She proceeded to eat them with a knife and a fork, methodically removing all the rice and pushing it around her plate for the entire meal. He was fascinated and appalled. They did not go out a second time.

When you order, choose something simple and easy to eat—nothing messy, like pasta, or that will require too much attention. A perfect choice would be grilled asparagus, a petit filet, and mashed potatoes. Yes, you can eat potatoes on a date—you won't go to hell. But you should never order spinach or a salad; that's a given, because inevitably something green and unattractive will end up between your two front teeth.

If you really want to make an impression, order dessert. I think some women are afraid to admit that they have ever met a sweet, let alone ingested one. But a person who is confident and enjoys life orders a dessert every now and then—or, at the very least, offers to share one.

Now let me give you a little advice about conversation. We do things differently down in Dixie, and everyone can learn from that. In the South, there is a more traditional approach to what to talk about on a date. For example, you don't discuss money, religion, or politics. Northerners are likely to exchange verbal résumés: they ask what you do, where you live, who you work for, and they even discuss how much things cost. The first time I went to dinner with Arthur's business partners I was flabbergasted when they started talking about the buying and selling prices of their apartments. That would never happen in the South.

Southern girls don't really ask, or tell, you everything because they like to retain an air of mystery. They'll circle around by discussing who your family is, or how many brothers and sisters you have—because they know listening to someone speak can tell you as much about them as what they actually say. Life is not as aggressive down here as it is in places like New York. A date doesn't have to be an interrogation. Flirting is more important than administering the third degree, and Southern women definitely do that better.

I define flirting as giving all of your attention to the person you are with, using what I call the "Nancy Reagan gaze." This works on all sexes, by the way. You look at your date with rapt attention, as if every word is a pearl of wisdom. You smile. You laugh. You're encouraging. You're impressed. You're appreciative, even if the conversation is about pig cloning. There are certain warm gestures you can employ to punctuate your conversation. Touching a person's sleeve, for example, shows that you're fully engaged and doesn't come across as being sexual. A few tips from the Southern flirt's handbook…

◇ Keep it playful and wholesome—no vamping.
◇ Use flattery genuinely and liberally, without being **unctuous**.
◇ Laugh at yourself and at life. Merriment is infectious (in a good way).
◇ Be the person who can talk to anyone about anything, but don't babble.
◇ Use your eyes and hands expressively, and with a light touch.
◇ Watch your language.

Unctuous: excessively or ingratiatingly flattering.

Asking questions and letting men talk about themselves usually makes them think they've had a wonderful conversation. Is this sexist? No. Maybe a little retro, in an amusing *Sex and the Single Girl* way. But being attentive is an indication of good manners. And what's wrong with turning up the wattage and being bright, funny, lively, and having a sense of humor about things? No one wants to be around a sourpuss or a grouch, and I assume no one wants to be one.

When I started to write this book, I took a look at my old, dog-eared copy of *Sex and the Single Girl* because I recalled that author Helen Gurley Brown offered smart, snappy advice to women in the 1960s. She did, bless her heart—and this time I mean that sincerely! Some of her suggestions seem quaint now because a single, independent woman is not the **rara avis** she was almost sixty years ago. There are a lot of references to premarital sex (remember that?), capri pants, and "man-snares." But I like the way she emphasizes the importance of one-on-one contact, or the classic date.

Rara avis: rare bird, a rare person or thing.

Like Helen, I want to revive the old-fashioned picnic as the best setting for Advanced Dating: a casual, yet captivating followup to exploratory drinks and the first dinner. Think Warren Beatty and Natalie Wood in *Splendor in the Grass*. What could be more romantic than a basket packed with food that is (or appears to be) homemade? My picnic basket, which I've had for ages and is probably considered vintage at this point, was made by Asprey & Sons of London and is outfitted with fine china and silverware. But you can find wonderful alternatives at **PicnicTime.com**. Their "Romance" basket comes with everything you need, including a corkscrew. Or, if you prefer, you can buy an empty basket and add your own decorative tin

A Southern Charm Christmas.

plates, plastic stemware that looks like crystal, silverware with wooden handles, and big linen napkins.

For a foolproof menu, include the classics: cold fried chicken, a cheese selection with a baguette, brownies, chilled wine or champagne, or mason jars filled with lemonade. Avoid anything with mayonnaise, because it spoils.

A Fine Showmance

Aside from my many years of personal experience, how do I know so much about finding a partner and maintaining a relationship? These days, one of the ways I stay up to date is by observing the mating rituals of my costars on *Southern Charm*. Whitney's in a class by himself because he's my son, of course. Cameran is happily married to her adorable husband, and Craig is with Naomi. But Landon, Kathryn, Shep, and Thomas are perfect examples of singles who could benefit from my advice. After all, no one wants to end up being a "shameless **strumpet**."

Landon, a beautiful young woman inside and out, doesn't know how beautiful she is. Because her first marriage ended in divorce, she's a little fearful and uncertain of how to move forward. As I like to tell her, get over the past and move on. When I knew my marriages were over, it was onward and upward, no looking back for me. No man is worth crying over! As trite as it sounds, I always think that things happen for the best—or at least I make them *be* for the best.

Strumpet: one of Shakespeare's favorite words to describe a woman of low repute.

Last season, Landon confessed to Shep that she was in love

with him. That didn't go well. But I applaud her for taking a chance—it may not turn out the way she wants, but it is important to try. I'm also trying to impress upon her how important it is to have a life of her own. Never give the impression that you're dependent on anyone else for your happiness. People can smell desperation a mile away, and they run away from it. You want a partner, not a Saint Bernard with a keg.

Shep is a darling guy—I love his smile! But I could have told Landon that he's a classic Peter Pan who is not ready to commit to anyone yet. That's what makes his social media handle, @relationshep, so funny and ironic. As Landon says, Shep is like "a golden retriever. If another ball comes by he chases it." You know the type, and if you accept him as he is, you can have a wonderful time. But if you fall for a Shep, better check those expectations about love, commitment, and happily-ever-after at the door.

In my heart, I have a soft spot for Thomas, even though I've been pretty hard on him. There's no question that Thomas has been a bit of a **rake** with women. Thomas was running for office at the time, and I thought he should be on his best behavior. I told him to think twice about getting entangled with someone whose ambition in life seemed to be to become a baby mama. My words were: "Instead of impregnating twenty-one-year-olds, you might want to refocus, is all I'm suggesting." He didn't listen.

Rake: a man, usually an aristocrat, who is charming, witty, sexually irresistible, and morally reckless.

This whole "baby mama" thing is alien to me. In my day, if you got knocked up, you went to a home for unwed mothers and your parents changed their name and moved to Missoula. Now you get to star in a reality show.

After hearing about Kathryn and Thomas's hard-to-believe

second pregnancy and witnessing all the crazy drama and discord in their "relationship," I had to tell Thomas a hard truth. "In all my ancient years here on earth," I said, "I don't know anybody who had to have one paternity test, and you've had to have two." He needed an intervention.

When You Think You've Found the Right One... Think Again and Again!

What makes smart people turn into dummies when they fall in love? Remember Maya Angelou's brilliant words: "When people show you who they are, believe them." Even though love is blind, keep your eyes wide open and pay attention to a potential mate's words and deeds. I think these considerations are so important. What is his relationship with his parents? Someone who doesn't speak to his mother, for example, is not a good prospect.

Do you have interests in common? That sounds like a no-brainer, but in the early blush of a relationship, we sometimes forget that our similarities can be more important than our differences. Not to make this too complicated, but the similarities in question should be important ones, not just funny coincidences. When I met my second husband, Ed Fleming, we were amazed to learn that both our mothers were Colonial Dames and that we both loved to eat Spam. Essentially, a shared passion for canned meat was the basis for our marriage a few weeks later!

I'm also amazed by what couples *don't* talk about. They may know each other's preferences for a Starbucks, or a football team, without ever discussing the important subjects that define a serious relationship. Before you even think about making a commitment, these issues must be on the table.

Vital Questions to Ask…

◈ What are your financial goals?
◈ How do you like to spend money? A free spender and a tightwad are going to have serious problems down the road.
◈ What about having children? Yes? No? How many?
◈ Religion?
◈ How much time do you expect to spend with his friends/your friends? How much time do you expect him to spend with his friends? Are you okay with Boys' Night Out, if that's his routine? Same questions for you, if you're planning regular trips to Chippendales!

As I've said, you have to be a risk taker. But I'm a big believer in taking *calculated* risks. The odds are against you if you think you can spend the rest of your life with someone without addressing these important questions.

My friend Georgette is a lifelong entrepreneur and CEO of international corporations, a political activist, a philanthropist, and one of the strongest and most successful women I know. She has a remarkable understanding of how to build a vital and enduring relationship, which she outlined in her best-selling book, *The Feminine Force: Release the Power Within You to Create the Life You Deserve.* I asked her to share her thoughts.

ASK THE EXPERT

Georgette Mosbacher

You stress that being attentive is one of the most important tools in connecting with another person. What's the best way to communicate interest?

Look people straight in the eye, be a good listener, and sincerely engage.

What are the two questions to ask yourself when you meet someone potentially appealing?

Do they have a good sense of humor, and do they have good manners?

What does it mean to be "game," and why is it important?

Be openminded, adventuresome, and curious, and those qualities will present opportunities that otherwise would not be so apparent. You will have a better chance of meeting interesting people if you're a little out of your comfort zone.

Is compromising a sign of defeat or a way to build a successful relationship?

Compromising is never a sign of defeat, unless you're compromising your values, and then you're just defeating yourself.

Of course, the relationship I'm most interested in is Whitney's. I used to go to the trouble of checking out the women he dated to see if they were daughter-in-law material. I hoped for a beautiful girl with a PhD in art history—someone well educated, cultured, and charming. I mean, my mother required my *beaux* to be in the Social Register. Now, I've shortened the list of requirements for Whitney's dream girl: I'll settle for anyone who walks upright.

That's a bit of an exaggeration. Whitney has had some lovely young women (and I mean *lovely*) in his life—although there have been several dubious choices. There was the Russian oligarch's daughter who arrived at the house with twenty suitcases and a puppy. She handed me the dog and made it clear that I had a choice: watch it poop and pee all over the living room or take care of it. Then there was the Latvian model who strolled through the gardens with Whitney, and said, while looking at the pool cover, which had puddles from a recent rainstorm, "That pool is not very deep." And I've saved the best for last: the clueless model who walked into the house, admired my paintings, and then very earnestly announced that her favorite artist was "Moët!"

I try not to be too judgmental (emphasis on *try*), or put too much pressure on my son, although every parent wants his or her child to be in a committed relationship with the right person. Whitney has been enjoying a smorgasbord of women, but I'm sensing that he may be ready for the main course.

Whenever Whitney decides to settle down, I have four engagement rings from my past—and my mother's—so he can take his pick. You can never have too many engagement rings. I would like him to get married. Almost all of my friends have grandchildren. I'm still waiting, but what I've done in the meantime is adopt a lot of pets.

I've been married three times, so I feel uniquely qualified to give advice about romance to Whitney—and to anyone else who will listen. To me, in order to get the life you want, you have to take chances and be open to change. I ended up with Arthur, the love of my life, when I took a leap and accepted his sudden invitation to move to New York. You may suffer a broken heart or two (or three) along the way. But whenever a relationship doesn't work out, try again. My motto is "Eat, drink, and remarry"—and it has served me well!

Setting the Stage

Marvelous Mario!

DON'T BE FRIGHTENED BY THE WORD *DECORATING*. I LIKE TO think of it as setting the stage for the continuing story of your life. Whether your style is traditional, contemporary, formal, or even what I like to call "Early Red Lobster" (which was my assessment of the décor in the beach house Whitney rented a while back), your home should express who you are and how you like to live.

I've decorated many residences in my time, including Southerly, which had thirty rooms, and, as I've mentioned, I've had the benefit of a thirty-five-year relationship with the incomparable Mario Buatta, who has been dubbed the "Prince of Chintz" by his fans.

Mario, who's as charming and quick-witted as he is talented, was featured on an episode of *Southern Charm*. He came to Charleston to put the finishing touches on my bedroom. It was right after my beloved cat Rocky died, and Mario startled Whitney by suggesting that I place a delft jar containing Rocky's ashes on a decorative bracket over my bed. He thought that would be very Southern. Of course, he was kidding, but Mario's a decorator who understands how to make a room unique.

Thanks to our long-standing collaboration, I know there are tried-and-true design formulas that can help you to achieve the look you want. The trick is that the results should never *seem* formulaic. Even though I often take a traditional approach, I like my surroundings to have a certain **verve**.

If you want to think like a designer, your most important considerations are color, lighting, scale, and comfort. I think a walk through my double drawing room (most people would call it a living room) will illustrate my points. Every room starts with its wall color. As Mario says, "A can of paint can change everything." There's only one way to choose a color. Brush large samples of paint—and I mean *large*—onto the walls and pay attention to how they look at different times of day, as the light changes. After a week, you'll know which color you prefer, and if you can live with it. I've chosen low-key pastels, specifically a vibrant

> **Verve:** vigor and spirit, or enthusiasm.

shade of Benjamin Moore apple green, custom mixed by Mario, for my double drawing rooms. The color is uplifting and flattering, whether the day is sunny or cloudy, and it is soft and beautiful at night.

Each room in the house has its own color

and texture, which creates a certain **ambience**. The library has dark, lacquered, Chinese-red walls because it is supposed to feel intimate, like a jewel box. The hall, which I wanted to be light, airy, and spacious, has pale faux marble walls. And I use wallpaper in rooms throughout the house. The wall

> **Ambience:** the character and atmosphere of a place.

covering in my dining room is very special to me. Made by the historic French company Zuber et Cie, it depicts vibrant scenes from the Revolutionary War. I actually had it taken down from the dining room at Southerly and moved to Charleston. It reminds me of one of my ancestors, who served under George Washington. I'm always happy to introduce history to my surroundings.

Never underestimate the power of lighting. I consider it to be a form of theater because it establishes the mood of the room. Is it cheery? Romantic? Bright? Intimate? More importantly, how does it make you look? It should be flattering. Overhead lighting is the enemy because it creates lines and shadows in all the wrong places, especially on the face! In the evening, everyone looks best if there's a soft glow. That's why I love floor lamps and position them strategically around the room.

I love candlelight, but candlesticks are appropriate only in the evening. I've attended luncheons in broad daylight where there were lit candles on the table, and that's just silly. When you entertain, always make sure that new candles are burned down a little, or they'll look like props in a furniture showroom. Light them an hour before your guests arrive, and keep the wicks trimmed (before you light them) so they don't sputter. At the end of the evening, use a proper snuffer to extinguish them, so you don't blow the wax everywhere. If you end up with drops of wax on your dining room table, the best way to remove it is to let it harden and scrape it off with a credit card. I also like scented candles, which can be lit at any time. The bamboo candle by Nest has a clean and pleasant scent that works in any room.

Mario likes to spend a weekend in a client's home before he determines the best approach to furniture, layout, and overall design, because he wants to understand how their rooms are used. If you're doing your own decorating, think about how you really live, and be brutally honest, especially if you have children and/or pets. If the rooms where you entertain have to serve two purposes, there are beautiful indoor/outdoor fabrics that can withstand family room activity in a living room.

Whether you are buying new furniture, using what you own, or combining the two, try to envision the whole room. Furniture never stands alone. No matter how much you love a particular piece, it has to work in concert with everything else. What I learned from Mario is that the preferred layout for a drawing room/living room includes a white or pale sofa flanked by two comfortable club chairs, with a large, low, Chinese-style table—a coffee table, but one that is square. Place occasional tables (round ceramic garden stools work perfectly) next to the club chairs. Armchairs with legs can be added, so they can be moved around to accommodate guests who are having a conversation.

If the room is large enough to accommodate more than one sofa, this grouping can be repeated. Once your core arrangement is in place, you can add pieces for visual variety. You need to stagger furniture of different heights or the room will look boring. A tall chest or a bookcase (I like a Chinese secretary with shelves) will offset the shorter sofa and chairs. Mirrors add height, light, and give a room life. And don't forget gilt! On a mirror, lamp, or picture frame—wherever it is—a flash of gold will catch the eye.

Most of the furniture in this house was moved from Southerly, so it was a challenge to install the pieces to a new environment. The fact that they look as if they've always been here is testament to their endurance and versatility. Which brings me to the dreaded word, *antique*. Some people freeze when they hear it. I hate rooms that look as if they belong in a museum, but I do love a touch of "something old." Most Southerners do. We surround ourselves with reminders of the past because history is so important to us. And I love having something in a room that's older than me.

Nostalgia isn't the only reason to buy antiques. From a practical standpoint, antiques are usually better made than new pieces, or reproductions, and they are renewable. A chair may look like it's dead and buried, but a new fabric and a good upholsterer can bring it back to life. And antiques can be surprisingly affordable. Local auction houses and internet auction sites are great resources for deals. I buy china and silver on the internet all the time, usually late at night, and I've found wonderful bargains. Besides, who can resist an object with a great story?

Comfort is something I cannot emphasize enough. Whatever your price range is, whether you buy custom or off the rack, a sofa, a chair, or any kind of seating, has to be inviting— *inviting* is an important word. I like a sofa to be enveloping, with bountiful cushions and pillows that are usually filled with down. But one of my pet peeves is the sight of stiff, knife-edged pillows lined up like soldiers. They look staged and they feel uncomfortable.

Floors are very important. We don't think of them as adding or subtracting light from a room—but that is definitely the case in the Isaac Mikell House. Mario thought the house looked too somber, so he painted the entrance hall's dark wooden floor white, and had it stenciled with a pattern designed to look like a floor in an English country house. Now the space looks lighter and brighter, and more appropriate for a home in the South. The white painted floor in my bedroom, polished to a bowling alley finish (and crisscrossed with blue *trompe l'oeil* ribbons in the adjacent bathroom), serves a similar purpose. The room feels light and airy, like a sunny garden sanctuary.

Trompe l'oeil: visual illusion in art, especially as used to trick the eye into perceiving a painted detail as a three-dimensional object.

I don't know why people bother with rugs when painted floors are pretty, cleaner, and much easier to live with if you have allergies or pets. Rugs are tricky to select and even trickier to position and maintain. In a living room the rug should be neutral, with a small pattern, and should cover the area where the furniture is centered. My Stark carpet from the large drawing room at Southerly was too big for either one of the double drawing rooms in Charleston, but Mario cleverly had it cut in half, and the resulting pair of rugs look as if they were made to fit the two new spaces.

Given my background, I always think that art is one of the most important elements in any room. Hang what you love, whether it was created by a professional or one of your children, but only if it is framed or mounted. And be careful where you place it. Most people hang their art too high or too low. When I worked at the Smithsonian, I learned that the curators did it by eye. I do that too, but if you want to be more scientific about it, the rule most decorators and gallerists endorse is as follows: in a room with traditional eight-foot ceilings, hang your artwork so the center stands between fifty-six and sixty inches from the floor—which is approximately "eye level." If your ceilings are higher (mine are fourteen feet) you can take advantage of the extra space and hang your pictures a little higher to draw the eye up.

Curtains, if you have them, should be punctuation, not a

verb. They're eyesores if they overpower everything else in the room. Mario is famous for his curtains and he's done the most beautiful window treatments throughout the house. They're all wonderful, but I must confess that I fell in love with a set of gorgeous, over-the-top curtains he made for one of my New York apartments. They were "couture" curtains—mauve, peach, and pink taffeta panels trimmed in light-catching crystals. They made me feel like Scarlett O'Hara. In a pinch I could have pulled them down and worn them to the Costume Institute Gala.

Once you've mastered the basics, you can start adding all the wonderful decorative touches that express your individuality. The items you choose for your coffee table (I like a selection of books, a pair of candlesticks or hurricane lights, a decorative box, and something wacky like the new turtle bell I use to summon Michael) should be the things you collect and cherish. I'm always surprised when I go into a house or apartment and don't see any books or magazines. That's a big black mark if you come across as someone who never reads!

Potpourri in a decorative bowl is a lovely touch. It lasts for months if you turn it over and add another box, or refresh it with scented oil. My favorite brand is Agraria. Their Bitter Orange blend (nicknamed "Park Avenue Potpourri") is filled with flowers, herbs, and spices and the scent is distinctive yet subtle.

Word to the Wise

If your living room is indeed a living room, it's a place for socializing and conversation. Let's be old Millennium. No television, telephone, or tablets, please.

Bedrooms

I'm often asked to name my favorite room in the house. It's hard to say, but because I'm basically lazy, I love my bedroom and bathroom, especially my bathroom, where I have a Jacuzzi tub, a big-screen television, a fireplace, and a toilet enclosed in a cabinet so I don't have to look at it. My bedroom suite is my little corner of the world, my refuge from reality— although this is where I watch all my favorite reality shows. Some nights, especially after an exhausting day of shooting *Southern Charm*, I can't wait to retire to my room with dinner on a tray, the television remote, and a good book. I also like to entertain my dogs there. I have a beautiful blue toile dog bed, but they prefer mine.

It is perfectly acceptable for *your* bedroom to be a personal space where anything goes, but a guest room, if you have one, has to be held to a higher standard. It can't be the place where unwanted things—worn pillows and blankets, old furniture, and God knows what else—go to die. And let's face it, if your grown child's former room is filled with toys, posters, and commemorative shot glasses, it's not a place for guests, it's a memorial.

For the guest room, you have to step up your Southern hospitality and create an environment that makes your guests feel wanted and special. The basics include:

- ❖ A comfortable bed
- ❖ Clean, attractive linens. I recommend D. Porthault, or the best-quality, sparkling white sheets you can afford
- ❖ Fresh pillows (and they should be replaced every few years)
- ❖ An extra blanket, preferably soft wool or cashmere
- ❖ Good bedside lighting
- ❖ A comfortable chair
- ❖ Blackout shades and/or curtains
- ❖ A decorative pad and writing implements on a table by the bed
- ❖ A card printed with the house wifi information
- ❖ Books and current magazines
- ❖ Bottled water
- ❖ Bedside snacks, such as fresh fruit, candy, or individual bags of popcorn

The bathroom you've set aside for your guest, if you have one, is another place that should be spanking clean and hospitable. In addition to providing good lighting and a generous supply of towels, think about the toiletries you yourself have forgotten to pack when traveling. Any guest will be grateful to find:

- ❖ Small bottles of shampoo and conditioner
- ❖ Soap (a fresh bar in its wrapper)
- ❖ Toothpaste and disposable toothbrushes
- ❖ A disposable razor
- ❖ Face wipes (These handy makeup removers may save your linens. Many of my D. Porthault pillowcases have been destroyed by women who sleep in eye makeup. It never comes out!)

- ◈ Sample packets of moisturizer
- ◈ Nail polish remover and a nail file
- ◈ Tylenol
- ◈ A sewing kit
- ◈ Shower cap
- ◈ Scented candle and matches

When you have company, going the extra distance to make them feel welcome guarantees that they will be good company, in every sense of the word. Conversely, guests should be on their best behavior when staying in your home. I asked Michael to share a few insider thoughts about what makes a guest "good."

ASK THE EXPERT

Michael Kelcourse

What's one of the worst things a houseguest can do?
Don't leave wet towels on the floor or on the bed. Fold them neatly and place them on the tub. And turn off the lights when you leave a room.

Are guests being pesky when they ask for things?
A good guest politely informs the hostess about requests and problems. People are so afraid to ask for what they want. But if a house has a staff, we're here to give you what you want.

What to do when something breaks—hide it and hope no one notices?
Inform your hostess if you break something. We don't care—we just want to know so it can be fixed or replaced.

The Light on the Piazza

Charleston is blessed with a beautiful climate (except during the dog days of summer). Here, and throughout the South, outdoor space is considered an important extension of the home. We take our porches—we call them piazzas—and yards very seriously. They're great settings for lounging, loafing, entertaining, and of course, gossiping.

The Isaac Jenkins Mikell House has wraparound piazzas on the first and second floors. In keeping with the house's Italianate origins, I've planted Meyer lemon trees in large Tuscan pots and positioned them so they can be seen from inside the house. When the lemons are hanging from the branches, I feel as if I am living in a Palladian villa in Italy! This beautiful tiled space has been the setting for many a *Southern Charm* moment, including the photograph on the cover of this book.

Below the piazza, the walled garden features pea-gravel-covered paths, boxwood hedges, statuary, a Greek revival dog house (and sometimes five frisky dogs), spectacular water lilies that bloom day and night, white camellias, and olive trees. I had an amazing crop of olives last year but didn't know what to do with them. I was excited about the possibilities until I discovered that an olive has a long, long way to go before it's ready for a martini glass.

If you have access to any outdoor space—a yard, a porch, a deck, a balcony—think like a Southerner and transform it into a retreat where you and friends can relax for a tall drink and a long chat. You'll come to regard it as the best "room" in the house. Define the area with potted trees, planters, and flowers—bougainvillea is a quintessential Southern choice. Add a French market table and chairs, candles, linen cocktail napkins, and wicker furniture. Then bring out the sweet tea or the bourbon slushies (recipe to follow) and settle in for a leisurely visit, Southern style.

Sean Brock, the James Beard Award–winning chef at Charleston's Husk restaurant, says, "If you sit on the porch long enough, you finally start telling the truth."[1] He's absolutely right. Many *Southern Charm* truths—the good, the bad, and the ugly—have come to light right here on my piazza.

The Collector in You

From art to antiques to Steiff animals, I surround myself with objects I love. But collecting doesn't have to be a one-percenter's game, nor does it have to turn a house into a hoarder's paradise. I'm as enthusiastic about Steiff stuffed animals as I am about seventeenth- and eighteenth-century needlework, as evidenced by the plush zoo that surrounds my Christmas tree. The secret is to arrange and display these collections in unexpected places and in eye-catching ways.

One of my best assemblages can be seen on the curved wall overlooking the staircase in the main hallway, where I hang my collection of eighteenth- and nineteenth-century silhouettes. My parents owned a few silhouettes when I was a child, and I had one done of Whitney when he was three. But it wasn't until I became an art advisor that I paid closer attention to the genre and started collecting them in Europe.

They have such an interesting backstory. Originally, a silhouette—a profile traced onto and cut from black paper—was an inexpensive alternative for people who couldn't afford to com-

---

1. Ligaya Figueras, "Art of the Porch Party," *Atlanta Journal Constitution*, June 26, 2016, E10.

mission painted portraits. They were called *portraits* à *la Silhouette* after Étienne de Silhouette, a notorious eighteenth-century French official who was famous for being a cheapskate. I found the best ones on the Left Bank in Paris and at antique fairs in London.

Arthur, who was a serious collector of museum-quality art, thought that silhouettes were great fun. One of our favorite activities was hunting for art and antiques together. Wherever we were—in

America or in Europe—we would wear ourselves out visiting dealers, galleries, auctions, and flea markets. It was almost more fun when we came across hidden treasure in unlikely places, such as a tag sale in a church basement. We found many silhouettes on these excursions.

My collection has many different kinds of silhouettes: some are cut out of paper, some are painted directly on glass; a few are sculpted in plaster; some are embellished with color, or gilt; some are painted on reverse glass; and two very unusual ones, which depict scenes in a royal court, were made by the queen of Portugal. The most valuable silhouette in my collection, and my favorite, depicts George Washington. To date, it's the only silhouette of him that was done from life. It was signed by the artist, Samuel Folwell.

Have I mentioned my obsession with antique French clocks? I think every mantel looks better with one, especially in rooms with high ceilings. Made of gilded bronze, with intricately designed figures, the clocks were manufactured in France in the eighteenth century. I'm always ready to pounce on an irresistible one at auction.

Arthur and I also shared a passion for antique silver. S. Kirk and Son presterling "coin" is the popular silver of the old South, and the preferred choice of traditional belles for their trousseaus. But I always preferred "Lap Over Edge," a stunning sterling pattern created for Tiffany & Co. In my opinion, Lap Over Edge, which was designed by Charles Grosjean in 1880, is the epitome of fine silver, despite the fact that it was made in the North. The pattern is in the Japanese style, with butterflies, berries, gourds, and other elements from nature. Arthur had amassed a huge collection of Lap Over Edge, but lost a substantial part of it in a divorce settlement. When we married we pooled our silver collections, and I still treasure it today.

My most whimsical "collection" is in my first-floor powder room, where I display a selection of perfume bottles for guests to sample. I confess that I wear only one perfume: Muguet by Guerlain, which is a light, floral fragrance infused with lily of the valley. Every year Guerlain invites a renowned artisan—a jeweler, a ceramicist, a sculptor—to create a limited-edition bottle, which is fabulously expensive and sells out immediately. I buy it, but, ironically, I always transfer the perfume into one of my pretty antique bottles because I prefer to apply my scent with an atomizer. There's something very feminine about spraying perfume the old-fashioned way and walking through a cloud of scent.

Since I never stray from my signature Muguet, I came up with a clever way to share the perfumes I get as gifts or samples. I line them up on a table in the first-floor guest bathroom, where they look beautiful and prove to be *very* tempting. Every woman loves the opportunity to try a new fragrance.

You really can call anything a "collection." I save invitations I've received over the years and keep the prettiest and most meaningful ones in a large decorative bowl on a console in my office. Some invitations are works of art, with elaborate engraving and calligraphy, while others bring back happy memories. Either way, I enjoy seeing them and remembering the stories that go with them.

I feel the same way about antique books. I have a complete set of first editions by P. G. Wodehouse, and other authors. I am always adding to my extensive collection of art books. And, I love my books about the South, especially the rare ones from my parents' library in Virginia.

I seem to be starting new collections all the time. When I was in India, I went crazy for elephants and brought back a procession of carved and embellished wood figures that will have a place of honor on my dining room table. Then I bought at auction a beautiful antique Dresden elephant Christmas ornament for my tree. I love alligators, monkeys, rabbits, and pugs in any form. My miniature china pugs are threatening to take over the house, just like my *real* dogs. I have everything from a rare, hand-painted eighteenth-century box depicting a pug to a pug on wheels that Mario bought in a drugstore. Collect what's important to *you*, regardless of its monetary value, and find a lovely way to showcase it. That's the best way to add personality to your home.

#pugsnotdrugs

Finding Your Style

If you're insecure about your sense of style, or feel that it's still evolving, don't be afraid to copy people you admire. Read shelter magazines—my favorites are *Architectural Digest*, *World of Interiors*, and *Veranda*—and start a file of what you like. Pictures can be inspiring. I've always enjoyed reading books by interior designers and studying up about the objects that interest me. There are so many resources available today, especially on the internet. Barbara Guggenheim, an important art advisor and a close friend for thirty-five years, has written an indispensable book about furnishing your home without having to leave the house. *Decorating on eBay: Fast and Stylish on a Budget* tells you how to find the pieces you want, and at the best price.

And then there's Mario, who always knows best. Even if you can't hire him, you can read his wonderful book, *Mario Buatta: Fifty Years of American Interior Decoration*, which is an enormous source of inspiration.

ASK THE EXPERT

Mario Buatta

What's the most common mistake people make when decorating their homes?

It's so easy to get scale and proportion wrong. Furniture ends up being too big or too small. I like to compare a room to a garden, where all the flowers and trees grow at different levels. Approach a room like a puzzle and give yourself time to think—eventually the right answers will present themselves.

What happens when a new design trend comes along? Does a room have to adapt?

The way I think never changes. Forget about instant gratification. You can't treat decorating as fashion—it's not like a dress you can push to the back of the closet. A great room is an investment in time and money, and if you do it correctly the first time, chances are you will never get tired of it.

What's the best way to prevent a room from looking stale?

A room is not a still life. Keep it fresh and up to date with flowers and living plants. Also, switch the books and objects you keep on your tabletops a few times a year—and, most importantly, display things you love and that bring you happiness.

Good Housekeeping

BECAUSE I HIRE PROFESSIONALS TO TAKE CARE OF MOST EVERY-thing, I'm not considered someone who knows much about housekeeping. But the truth is, you cannot manage a house properly unless you've learned how to do things for yourself. My mother, who had a system and a schedule for everything, taught me well. I have very definite ideas about the best way to maintain a house, even if I'm not the one to execute them. For that, I rely on Michael, the butler.

For most people, the butler is the fastidious overseer on *Downton Abbey*, or the one "whodunit" in a game of *Clue*. Fans of *Southern Charm* are fascinated by Michael and want to know who he is and how he spends his time, other than serving me a frosty martini on a silver tray. As I've said before, Michael is my majordomo. He's in charge of the house and everyone who works there, whether it's a cook, a housekeeper, a laundress, a gardener, or a pool person. Anyone. The International Butler

Academy (yes, there is one), compares the modern butler to a Swiss Army knife—a butler has to be a problem solver, first and foremost, then knowledgeable, organized, and have the ability to multitask. Michael has all of these virtues.

You want the people who work for you to be dedicated and professional. But there are other considerations. A butler is in your home constantly and sees you every day, and in every situation. He knows all of your **foibles** and secrets, so your relationship has to be based on trust, mutual respect, and a sense of humor. On top of that, you have to like him. Eventually, if all goes well, he becomes a member of your family. That's Michael, the consummate professional, the soul of discretion, and the perfect straight man to my often outrageous one-liners.

> **Foible:** a minor weakness or eccentricity in someone's character.

Since many of you have asked, Michael was born and raised in Michigan. As a child, he enjoyed reading and watching television, and even as a youngster, he was fascinated by stories of the Gilded Age—the time between the Civil War and World War I, when American society was ruled by the Astors, the Vanderbilts, and other fabulously wealthy families. He attended college in Michigan and went to work in a nursing home—until it occurred to him that instead of caring for people who were sick, he could make a career out of looking after people who were well...and well-off.

It turned out to be difficult to find that kind of job in Michigan because there weren't enough rich people who maintained full-time domestics. Michael moved to New York, hoping to obtain a position in a private household. He found the ultimate Gilded Age employer in the elderly Mrs. Bostwick, who had eighteen servants in residence and ran her home the old-fashioned way. In addition to a full complement of cooks, maids, and other domestics, Mrs. Bostwick had three different chauffeurs—one for day, evening, and the weekend. There were two enormous residences—in Old Westbury and on Park Avenue—with the attendant responsibilities, including maintaining an impeccable household and serving meals and afternoon tea every day.

The family's ninety-year-old butler took Michael under his wing, and Michael was a quick study who prided himself on knowing what his employer wanted before *she*

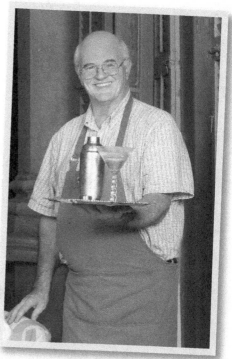

"It's time for my medicine!"

knew she wanted it. By the time I persuaded him to come work for me at Southerly, he was a first-class butler.

Initially, Michael was a little horrified when I broached the idea of leaving New York—the only place he had visited in the South was Palm Beach, and he didn't know a thing about Charleston. But he was a good sport about moving to a new city, a new climate (fortunately, Michael doesn't like snow), and a new home.

I'm set in my ways when it comes to running my household. Because my father was a physician, he was always waging war against germs. Here are some important cleaning routines that everyone should do, or have done:

◈ Once a month, saturate cotton pads with rubbing alcohol (or use antiseptic wipes) to clean

all the surfaces you touch regularly, including light switches, handles, doorknobs, telephones, and keyboards.
- ◈ Dusting always starts at the top, moves down, and is followed by vacuuming.
- ◈ Use sable brushes to dust the frames on paintings and a special brush by Redecker to dust books.

Regular dusting, waxing, and polishing make a house gleam. These are the preferred products in the Isaac Mikell House:

- ◈ Renaissance microcrystalline wax polish (which is used in the British Museum)
- ◈ Town Talk polish scented with lavender for the boudoir, because you don't want an industrial smell where you sleep
- ◈ Hagerty silver spray for silver photograph frames
- ◈ Wright's silver polish
- ◈ Murphy's oil soap for wood floors

And Michael adds this important tip—don't forget to clean your light bulbs!

Organization

When you do things in a haphazard manner, that's how they'll look and feel. I try to be very organized, especially when it comes to managing all the stuff we bring into our lives. Stay on top of it by maintaining an up-to-date inventory of your possessions. This is something I learned when I was studying art history. Works of art are catalogued with a provenance, which is a detailed record of ownership that proves authenticity or quality. But you don't have to be an art collector to keep **copious** records. The same process works whether you're storing information about an oil painting or a new flat-screen television.

Copious: exhibiting abundance or fullness, as of thoughts or words.

As soon as you buy something substantial, take a photograph and place the picture in a plastic sleeve in a binder, along with the receipt for the item and all the supporting information, including where and when you bought it. I store my hardcopies in large white three-ring binders because they look neat and unobtrusive on a shelf—and I keep a digital backup, just in case. Those of you who are really clever can take a digital photograph of the object and the receipt, tag it with the important details, and upload it to the cloud, or a record-keeping app such as Evernote. If you are the victim of a robbery, a fire, or any disaster, for that matter, you will have everything you need to make an insurance claim. Start right now and get into the habit of doing it every time you bring something important into the house. If you procrastinate, the job will be too big and you'll never do it.

My assistant, Joan, who can organize *anything*, offers some guidance.

ASK THE EXPERT

Joan DiPietro

What's the best way to organize household papers? Should a filing system be A–Z, or divided into categories (i.e., insurance, home improvement, etc.)?

I basically file A–Z, but some files such as insurance, health insurance, bills, and home improvements, are kept separate.

Do you have a special system for financial records? How do you keep income tax information organized and up to date?

For financial records, I just keep bank records together, and if it's a business account, once the account is reconciled, I make a copy for the accountant for year-end taxes.

Also, when I file bills, if they are not tax-deductible expenses I discard and file the current bill. However, certain bills I keep, including telephone and utilities bills. If you have more than one home and you get audited by the state, they will want those bills. I also record in a daybook all of Mrs. Altschul's activities and appointments. For the year-end taxes, I use a spreadsheet on the computer to record all tax-deductible expenses and send that to the accountant.

Do you have a system for opening and sorting mail?

As far as mail goes, I take care of it each day or it will pile up. I get rid of junk mail and shred all credit card requests, file bills in a bill file until I am ready to pay the bills, and place invitations in an invitation file according to date.

Let Me Entertain You

IT'S BEEN SAID THAT MY PARTIES WILL MAKE THE SOUTH RISE again, which is a lovely compliment. I was asked to write about entertaining because I know how to host a great party. Just this year, I was honored to be included on The Saloniere's list of the 100 Best Party Hosts in America. To be honest, it wasn't always that way! Let's go back in time to the 1960s, when I was a newlywed. Lon and I decided to have a dinner party in our new, modern apartment. We invited two or three couples, our best friends at the time. Almost all of us were in school with crazy schedules, so Saturday night was our time to relax and have fun.

I wanted to impress our guests. Since complicated, "gourmet" dishes were very popular, I decided to make beef stroganoff. I had been given a book called *If You Can Read, You Can Cook*, and I made the mistake of taking the title literally. I knew how to read—I was a graduate student, after all. But I was awfully cocky to think I could pull off a recipe that had so many steps. I definitely cut corners on the rest of the menu. We served sour cream and onion soup dip with chips for hors d'oeuvres (which I still serve today because it's really good). The house drink was that frat specialty bourbon and Coke. If you wanted to make it really redneck, you could put peanuts in it.

I'm sure that drink has been the downfall of many a hostess, and that night I was having so much fun that I got a little sloppy with the stroganoff recipe. I kept adding ingredients and it ended up very soupy, with pieces of meat floating on the top. One guest not-so-politely called it monkey barf. The noodles, a key part of the stroganoff, stuck together in clumps. Then, to add to the excitement, a dish towel caught fire and I had to stomp it out.

The rest of the evening was a blur. At some point I took all of my clothes off and got into bed. I vaguely remember our guests calling out their goodbyes as they left. They were probably starving and headed for the nearest diner. That was definitely the low point of my entertaining career. After that, I started watching Julia Child and taking it all more seriously.

I became a more experienced hostess, but whenever possible, I found novel ways to stay out of the kitchen. After we moved to Virginia, Lon decided that he wanted to entertain clients at home, in his "castle." My solution to that problem was to call the local Chinese restaurant, order a banquet of food, and serve it on my best china. Apparently, the sight of chicken chow mein, moo shu pork, and fried rice displayed on Spode or Minton, instead of in a little white box with a wire handle, is irresistible. Our guests couldn't get enough of it and, for some reason, thought that I was a brilliant hostess.

Thrilled with my ingenuity and success, I did the same thing with Mexican food—I ordered in takeout and plated it as elegantly as Dover sole meunière at La Côte Basque. If our guests were really lucky, they were treated to platters of fried chicken and corn bread, traditional Southern comfort food prepared by our housekeeper, and that's still one of my favorite meals. Lon, who was an expert on wine, always knew exactly what to pair with my whimsical menus. I think mixing the high and the low amuses people. Trying to be too fancy, formal, or correct can be a bore. You want your guests to relax and have fun.

I'd like to point out that one of the best hosts of all time was a Southerner. The great writer Truman Capote grew up in a small town in Alabama. In 1966, when he was living in New York, he conceived and executed the Black and White Ball, which is considered the most famous party in modern social history. Capote planned his ball the same way he wrote his blockbuster books *In Cold Blood* and *Breakfast at Tiffany's*: he agonized over every detail—the theme (a masked ball), the guest list (the who's who of all time), the dress code (black and white), the food (his favorites—spaghetti and chicken hash), the décor (minimalist—he said the people were the flowers). He mixed it up, high and low, and his budget—fifteen thousand dollars—was small, even for the time. As a result, we're still talking about that party today. The first lesson of entertaining is to be creative, to have a personal vision, and to dedicate the requisite time, effort, and resources to bringing that vision to life.

But let's clarify "resources." If you throw enough money at an event, you can recreate the Hall of Mirrors at Versailles, but that doesn't mean your guests will have a good time. I'm shocked by how much people spend, with the sole purpose of impressing their guests. But I'm never impressed by excess: all I can think about is what a waste of money it is. People are more likely to remember your party if you do something genuinely amusing. Creativity and wit always trump wretched excess.

For example, we read about the tens (and sometimes hundreds) of thousands of dollars celebrities spend on their children's birthday parties. Not long ago, a friend had a party to celebrate his son's first birthday. It was in a public park, and he brought in a little petting zoo. There were bunnies, chicks, and kittens. The kids loved it. The adults were charmed. And the birthday boy had more fun holding a baby animal than he would have had watching Cirque du Soleil in his back yard.

A Southerner's door is (almost) always open because we love to entertain at home. That's our favorite setting. New York is different. When I lived there, we often hosted dinners in restaurants, or bought a table at a charity event. Here, whether the occasion is fancy or casual—a holiday cocktail party or a down-and-dirty crab feast—we're likely to do it at home, which makes the undertaking more personal.

Raising the Bar

Since being Southern equals hospitality, I'm always prepared to offer a guest a drink. There are several standing bars on the first floor of my house—in the morning room (where the lady of the house used to meet with staff), the library, and the butler's pantry—and they come in handy for different kinds of entertaining. The correct way to set up a bar is to have an assortment of glassware, basic kinds of alcohol and mixers, and when we set up for a party, fresh lemons, limes, and doggie swizzle sticks, which are very cute. Michael recommends having tons and tons of ice—his formula is eight ounces for every guest. At parties I serve only white wine, rosé, and champagne—never red, just in case there's a spiller in the group.

Our working bar is in the butler's pantry. It's Michael's stage, where he makes his famous cocktails, and I must say his performance always gets rave reviews. There's an ice machine, a small wine cooler, a big wine refrigerator in the adjacent room, an electric corkscrew, other bar hardware and equipment, and a variety of glassware.

Michael likes to have a range of ingredients on hand in case someone wants an unusual drink—we keep onions for Gibsons, cherries for Manhattans, and olives for martinis. Stock two or three kinds of vodka because everyone is so fussy, and a few brands of gin. It's nice to have rye and several good bourbons— Southerners like Bulleit for a mixed drink and Pappy Van Winkle if you're serving it straight up. Select your alcohol on the basis of taste, not price. Yes, they should be good quality, but the most expensive brand is not necessarily the best. We always keep a very good dry vermouth, orange bitters, and regular bitters, in case we get a request for a champagne cocktail.

The bar in the library is for after-dinner drinks. When I have parties I fill the decanters with brandy and cognac, and make sure the appropriate glassware, including snifters for brandy and cordial glasses, are on the bar cart. The library has become a hangout for Whitney and his friends, who come in and smoke cigars and drink brandy until the wee hours. Whitney keeps two humidors stocked with Cuban cigars (with distilled water in the bottom to keep them moist.)

I just gave Whitney a beautiful Christmas present—an antique crystal decanter in the shape of cockatoo sitting in a silver cage and surrounded by shot glasses. Actually, it is more of a present for me, but he's so hard to buy for that I'm pretending it's for him. I'll keep it until he gets married. Meanwhile, I'm getting thirsty with all this talk—is it five o'clock yet?

The Infamous Dressing Drink

Well this seems like a good time to talk about "taking your medicine." People think I drink martinis all day long. I wish! I don't drink *that* much, but I do enjoy a perfect martini every day at 5 p.m., and I come by my appreciation for the drink honestly.

My parents, who had a great love story, shared a charming tradition when I was growing up. Unlike children today, I did not go to restaurants with my mother and father at night, spread my coloring books on the table, and make annoying noises. I had supper in the kitchen, a bath, homework, and then I was off to bed. Meanwhile, every evening, my parents enjoyed an interlude they regarded as "their time." Before dinner, they sat together and chatted over a shaker of martinis. I thought it was so adult and cosmopolitan, like something out of a Nick and Nora Charles movie. I remember once woofing down a tiny drop when the glasses came back into the kitchen, and I liked it.

Ed Fleming, my second husband, was related to Ian Fleming, the writer who created James "shaken, not stirred"

Michael's Perfect Martini

Place gin and vermouth (ratio 1 to 2, or 2 to 3) in a shaker. Fill a shaker with ice. Let sit.

Using the Lewis ice mallet and bag, crush a new batch of ice into splinters and place in a glass almost to the top—add an olive or a twist of lemon. Give the shaker two or three good shakes (if filming, do it with a flourish!) and pour into the glass.

Sip appreciatively.

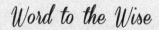

Word to the Wise

You're going to love this. There's a reason why I use the term "dressing drink." Being a host, or a guest, comes with certain responsibilities. When I'm having company, I know that all of my attention will go to my guests, and I'll be too busy to sip a cocktail or a glass of wine. So, while I'm upstairs, putting the finishing touches on my toilette, I enjoy a leisurely "dressing drink," a martini or a bourbon slushie. By the time I put on my lipstick, I feel as if the party has started!

Bond *and* who apparently made the best martini in the world. Ed inherited the family talent. What makes a martini perfect? I depend on Michael, who has the magic martini touch, to smash ice with a mallet, in a special Lewis bag, no less, to ensure the perfect consistency. Then he shakes precise proportions of gin, vermouth, and ice, pours it into a glass, and garnishes it with olive or lemon, depending on my mood.

I prefer Beefeater gin—it's not the most expensive brand, but I find it to be less biting than other kinds. I'm joking when I refer to my martini as "medicine," but gin is actually full of botanicals, including juniper, lemon peel, coriander seed, almond, Seville orange peel, orris root, liquorice root, angelica root, and angelica seed. Vodka martini lovers take note: vodka comes from the lowly potato, while gin is elegant and healthy. For vermouth, I prefer Boissiere, which is dry, white, and French.

When Michael goes away on vacation, I'll abstain. Or if I'm at a restaurant or a bar and the martini is below my standards, I will not drink it. Period. Because I have no interest in an inferior martini. Recently I was interviewing for a second butler. I don't have a husband right now, so I've been filling up the house with butlers, and as far as I'm concerned, you can't have too many of them. I explained that top-notch martini making was one of my chief requirements for employment. I don't care if a candidate is a serial killer as long as he can make a great martini. Luckily, Jesse passed the test and I hired him on the spot.

As you've probably gathered, I'm all in favor of drinking—as long as it's not carried to extremes—and that can be a matter of personal interpretation. My prescribed dosage is that women should have one drink a day, whether they like it or not, and men can have two, and I got that advice from my doctor at the Mayo Clinic. Whitney has a broader approach. He calls alcohol "chicken soup for the soul," an observation I keep threatening to needlepoint on a pillow. But let me remind you that after one two drinks too many, you don't even taste it, so what's the point? My rule for determining when a person's had enough

Michael's Bourbon Sour (Slushie)

- ℽ 2 ounces of whiskey sour mix (preferably Master of Mixes)
- ℽ 1 ounce bourbon

Blend in electric blender with desired amount of ice. Place in a goblet. Finish with a bourbon-soaked cherry and a slice of orange.

to drink is what my friend at @welovepataltschul calls the test for "The Louboutin Lush." If you are incapable of walking up stairs in high heels—that applies to men and women—you've had too much. And if you take off your heels to feign sobriety, that's cheating.

Southerners, of course, should get a free pass when it comes to drinking. Yankees don't understand leisure and the casual cocktail, so I think it is totally different for them. It's hot down here, and cooling off with a drink is a Southern tradition we're all doing our part to keep going.

I thoroughly enjoy planning all kinds of gatherings, large and small, with one notable exception. The meal you will never sit down to in my house is brunch. I don't even like the word, and I don't like having to function early in the morning. I think it's uncivilized. The rest of the time, be my guest for dinner, cocktails, and any other excuse I can think of to entertain!

Dinner Parties

Hosting a dinner party is like trying to write a **haiku**, or more accurately these days, a tweet. You're working with a limited amount of time, space, and "characters." But that's precisely what I love about an intimate evening in the dining room—it's edited for maximum impact.

> **Haiku:**
> a traditional Japanese haiku is a three-line poem written in a five/seven/five syllable count.

Sitting together at the table for a meal was a ritual in our family. But one of the problems with society today is that we're always eating on the run. That makes a dinner party a special occasion.

Sometimes I have a reason to entertain—a friend is in town, or I haven't seen someone in a long time. Other times I just feel like having a dinner party. I usually invite eight to ten people, and I put a lot of thought into assembling a lively group. I think of a few "adults," people of the same age who know each other, or who might enjoy meeting for the first time. Then I throw in some younger people and a few Southern eccentrics. I like an eclectic mix. Once I've determined my guest list, I pick up the phone and call each one, which sounds so retro in our email/e-vite world. Conversing with a human reminds you why you wanted to invite the person in the first place.

Of course, the best-laid guest lists can go awry, or at least unexpectedly. I invited a married couple to come to a dinner party and they accepted. God knows why. It turned out that I was the only person on the planet who didn't know they were getting a divorce. They sat at my table and snarked and sniped at each other all night, like heavyweight champions. After our initial discomfort, we all settled in to watch the fight. It was great theater! My friends are still talking about it.

I have a philosophy about the dining room, or dining area. It starts with a good table. The Jeffersonian approach calls for the table to be round because it is more democratic. Without a "head" or "foot," everyone is equal. And it shouldn't be too large. It may sound counterintuitive, but guests should be crammed together, rubbing elbows, so to speak. People will be more talkative if they are close together—it has something to do with herding. Michael considers table-setting an exact science. He walks around the table measuring the distance from the edge to the plate. He recommends leaving an inch.

I use a diagram in my Leathersmith of London's hostess book to come up with a seating plan, and when I set the table, I use place cards to indicate where the guests will sit. I have an

Whitney, Thomas, Craig, and Shep—my Southern gentlemen.

eclectic collection of placecard holders, including a set of little pigs. And I treasure a collection of antique jockey figurines I purchased at auction from the estate of John Hay Whitney. My rule is to split up couples and individuals with the same profession—no lawyers sitting next to lawyers, or they'll talk shop all evening. But I don't subscribe to the precept of alternating boy/girl/boy/girl in a seating arrangement. If I think two people will find each other interesting I don't care about gender. In fact, I enjoy hosting all-male dinner parties. I often did that when Arthur was alive—we'd have dinner, and then the "boys" would go off to play poker. Now it's become a tradition on *Southern Charm*. Whitney, Shep, Thomas, Craig, and sometimes JD, are the core group.

When I decorate a table, I try to think like a set designer. I want it to be beautiful, but I also want to create an atmosphere, so I start with a basic setting and then add the touches that will bring the table—and the dinner—to life. If I am hosting a formal dinner, I use a linen tablecloth. Otherwise, the table is

159

set with linen placemats, with specially cut felt mats underneath to hold them in place. For everyday meals and luncheons, I use rush mats. My linens are custom made in Madeira, Portugal, by Léron Linens. Because I'm so finicky about how my table linens are maintained and stored, they're always ready.

Word to the Wise

Here's the best way to store linens: napkins and placemats should be laundered and pressed, and each set (holiday, white lace, floral, etc.) is placed on its own heavy cardboard sheet (which we buy at an art supply store), and labeled. I don't have to remind you how important it is to have a good labeling machine (my new one, the Dymo LabelWriter 450, is very easy to use because it connects to my computer). When the table is ready to be set, each board is easily retrieved, so it's like having a well-ordered library of selections. I keep tablecloths (after they have been laundered and pressed) in drawers lined with scented paper.

I'm very fussy about my napkins; I want them to be grand. Vintage linens tend to be more generous in size than modern ones, which are too skinny for me, and the best place to find them is online and at flea markets. My greatest coup was when I came across a quantity of large linen napkins with an embroidered crown in the corner. They had been made for the King of Bavaria. I was so excited when I found them—I bought tons and I use them all the time. They're real conversation pieces, because they're unusually large. At my table, with one of these napkins in your lap, you could gut a deer and you wouldn't get a drop of blood on you.

I know it's a luxury, but I have several sets of silver and china—some casual, some formal—and I use them depending on the occasion, my mood, the season; there are many variables. Menu is a practical consideration. For example, I won't serve meat on a dish that has gilt, or an embossed design, because the blade of a knife might scratch it. It's better to serve soft food on highly decorated china.

The one thing that irritates the hell out of me is chargers—you know, the oversized plate that serves no purpose but to hold a plate? It all started when Salomé asked for the head of John the Baptist on a charger, which is not what you want to think about when you're dining. I think they are pretentious, totally unnecessary, and silly. You'll *never* see one on my table, and I hope I never see one on yours.

I have a varied collection of crystal for different drinks and occasions—Waterford, Baccarat, William Yeoward—and some great antiques, including European glasses with dogs etched on them. The glass I'm passionate about is the old-fashioned champagne coupe, the wide-mouthed champagne glass that used to be popular. Supposedly, its rounded shape was inspired by Marie Antoinette's breasts, which may or may not have been used to create the mold. They fell out of fashion in the 1970s (the glass, not the breasts) when it was thought that the narrower flute did a better job of preserving the bubbles. I think the coupe is much more elegant and festive than the flute, and honestly, I drink champagne so fast that I never have to worry about preserving the bubbles.

My centerpieces range from formal to whimsical. For a

formal dinner, a low floral arrangement is a good choice, but I avoid flowers that give off too strong a scent. I find that a clever assortment of objects can be eye-catching, too. When I hosted a dinner to celebrate the arrival of Thomas's new baby boy, I called it a "Blue and White" dinner (because the color blue is for boys of all ages). With the help of my friend, Carolyne Roehm, the author of twelve books on décor and entertaining, I gathered blue and white porcelain jars from all over the house and arranged them as my centerpiece. They looked beautiful!

ASK THE EXPERT

Carolyne Roehm

Let's talk about flowers. What can you do if you don't have a garden? Where should we buy flowers? What's the best way to achieve that beautiful, "just-picked" look? And can you tell us your tricks for transforming the lowly carnation or sunflower into a superstar?

Whenever I lecture, I like to say, "There are no bad flowers, only people who have no ability to use them correctly." In my first book, I campaigned for the return of the carnation and other so-called old-fashioned, or "boring," flowers. These lovely pariahs have been ostracized, or overlooked, and for no good reason. People assume that I just reach into my big garden of exotic blossoms when I make an arrangement, but the truth is that I use all kinds of flowers—even alstroemeria gladiolas, and marigolds—from everywhere! The grocery store is a big source—also Trader Joe's, Whole Foods, and I like potted plants from Lowe's or Walmart. Many wholesale markets will sell to nonprofessionals toward closing time.

If there are no flowers, I create centerpieces with fruit,

greens, weeds, piles of shells or nuts, or whatever. If nothing is handy, I pull out a soup tureen, or an object that I love, and place it on my table.

You're a big believer in movable feasts. Can you talk about how you have liberated the table from the dining room?

I love to entertain where the view is pleasing. If it is summer and my rose garden is in bloom, I set my table there. If it is cold and

Carolyne and Chauncey.

snowy I set my table next to a favorite fireplace. I no longer have many dining rooms—my rooms do double duty, such as here in Charleston. The library is turned into the dining room, or the greenhouse is transformed into a dining room—the same with my stable. Anything goes. Unless you entertain all the time, the dining room is just an unoccupied, rather lonely, space that you walk through on your way to someplace else.

When you entertain, you have an incredible eye for detail and use the table to tell a story. How can someone learn to create a more expressive setting?

What's the first step? Study examples of work you like, pull out photos from magazines, or take screenshots of online images, and keep a file. Sources of inspiration are limitless— the season, a new object you have acquired for your table, the selection from your garden or the flower market, the interests of your guests. Have an inquisitive eye and see where it leads you. But if presentation is not important to you, find another way to make your entertaining unique. Maybe you're a marvelous cook, or you curate the best music!

What about the people who didn't inherit their great-grandmother's china and silver? Where can they shop for affordable table settings and what should they look for?

So many people of great style did not inherit things—and even if they had, chances are they might not choose to use them. I'm a perfect example. My grandmother loved many Victorian-influenced decorative items. While I learned so much from her and we shared so many interests, our styles were not the same. When I was younger and longed for beautiful things (but had no money), there were few places to shop. Today, the availability of stylish, yet affordable, glasses, dinnerware, flatware, and other decorative objects is staggering. You can go to Crate and Barrel, Williams Sonoma Home, Ballard, and even Target. I just bought some serving trays, wrapping paper, and Christmas decorations from Lowe's!

For those who are color-wheel challenged, what are the two color combinations guaranteed to make a table pop?

My go-to combination would be blue and white, and I love these colors so much that I wrote a book about them. Celadon is also a good choice, because green is a predominant color in nature. Or, if you want to keep it simple, use all white, and make texture the chief design element. I could go on forever on this subject…

———————

Then there was the memorable *Southern Charm* stag dinner when I decorated the table with plastic alligators arranged in compromising sexual positions. I couldn't help myself. It was too good!

In addition to placecards, I like to put something playful at each guest's setting. Sometimes I order specialty chocolate creations from Christophe Artisan Chocolatier here in Charleston. For one dinner party I selected Louboutin high heels for the ladies—and they looked exactly like Louboutins, except they were edible—and chocolate cigars for the men. At my Indian dinner, I ordered chocolate elephants.

On other occasions I use custom-made cookies as placecards, and have the person's name written in icing. Here's a great tip: You can find cookie cutters in any shape or size, everything from the state of Texas to a tiara, at **cookiecutters.com**. Bake them yourself, or, if you're like me, bring the cookie cutters to your favorite bakery (I use the Sugar Bakery in Charleston), and they can make cookies to your specifications. I often have alligator-shaped cookies wearing appropriately colored ribbons at my parties. And for one of my *Southern Charm* stag dinners, I decorated the table with what I called "male chauvinist pigs" made out of marzipan, which I found on the internet. These treats double as decoration and dessert.

When I plan a menu, I'll choose fun food over fancy food every time. You don't have to serve a standing rib roast or a Cordon Bleu dish to your guests. Give them good old-fashioned comfort food—something like lasagna and salad, or meatloaf, followed by cookies and candy—which they will appreciate much more than a complicated dish that kept someone in the kitchen all day. At my dinner for Thomas I served "Mad Men" comfort food—shrimp cocktail and that old glamour puss cherries jubilee flambé—because it seemed appropriately male. The people, not an extravagant menu or an elaborate décor, make the party.

I always have someone to serve at my dinner parties. But if you are doing it yourself, arrange the food on a sideboard (every dining room should have one) so guests can get up and help themselves. If it is a very casual meal, you can serve "family style," with platters on the table.

One of the questions I'm asked most frequently is: how do I stay composed and charming when the company is not? As viewers know, some of the dinner parties on *Southern Charm* turn into trainwrecks, with guests abandoning the food and running for their lives. These situations tend to be extreme. Remember the time Thomas hosted a dinner and managed to insult every single guest before the first course was served? This kind of madness never happens at my house. Everyone knows that they have to clean up nicely and mind their manners at Miss Patricia's, or else! Nonetheless, dinner parties definitely present some challenges, because guests are unpredictable. The evening could be pleasant, explosive, or a snoozefest. You never know what will happen.

A hostess (or a host) is a ringmaster. At your circus, you have to pay attention to everything, including the conversation at large. Are your guests playing nicely with each other? I find that the two most incendiary topics are politics (especially these days) and religion. Lively discourse is one thing, but never get into an argument socially about these subjects. As much as I admire diversity and respect other people's opinions, I refuse to get into a fight, because you're never going to change anyone's mind at a dinner table.

What can you do to avoid **fisticuffs**? Say something like, "Now that's an interesting observation," and immediately go on to a neutral subject. *People can't force you to engage.* A good diversion is to ask a question: "I've been meaning to ask you about your..." and fill in the blank. Your trip to the islands. Your new dog. Your son's wedding. Your French lessons. *Anything* to head off a violent disagreement. And keep a note of humor in your voice.

Fisticuffs: a fight with the fists.

In the dining room you're always amused, never angry. That's the essence of Southern charm.

Too much drama is one problem, but the opposite is no better. So, what do you do about a dinner party with no pulse? You know, the one where the silence is deafening, when all you hear is the sound of the silverware hitting the plate? If your guests are not doing their job by being witty and fascinating, you have to help them along.

I think that obvious opening **gambits** ("What are the three foods you would bring to a desert island?") can seem contrived. Since you've followed my advice about reading and you're up to date on current events and popular culture, you should have plenty to say. At one of my last dinner parties I mentioned that Charleston had been voted the number one city in the world, and that inspired a spirited discussion about whether or not it deserved the honor. This is why I suggest reading the *National Enquirer*. No joke, it is a great source for the latest believe-it-or-not stories.

Gambit: a remark intended to start a conversation.

Everyone enjoys talking about food, books, travel, local events, and discoveries of some sort. But in my decades of

Word to the Wise

When you are at a seated dinner, speak to the guest on your right while eating the first course, and turn to the guest on your left for the second course. This custom is called "turning the table." It is an excellent habit that prevents anyone from being left out of the conversation.

socializing, I've found that the foolproof way to spark a conversation is to let a person talk about himself, which never takes much coaxing. It works at dinner parties just as well as it works on dates. I remember being seated next to a famous nuclear physicist at a dinner and wondering, *What the heck will I talk to this man about?* As soon as I asked him to explain black holes, Foucault's pendulum, and anything else I could think of that related to his profession, we were off to the races. He never stopped talking, and he told his wife later that I was the best conversationalist.

We've all experienced that terribly awkward moment when a guest breaks something—*that* can stop any conversation dead

Word to the Wise

I've said it before, but device etiquette bears repeating. The rule used to be "Don't put your elbows on the table." Today, people (well, impolite people) have two iPhones on the table and maybe an iPad on the seat next to them. It has gotten out of control. I have asked guests to put away their cell phones, because there is nothing ruder than to sit with someone who is cutting their steak and checking their tweets. I think it is unacceptable behavior. Social media is an addiction, and a lot of people who would ordinarily be very courteous can be thoughtless and disrespectful because their perception of what is appropriate has gotten blurred. Phones should be put away and turned off.

THE ART OF SOUTHERN CHARM

in its tracks. Even if it's a precious antique, I clean it up and never make a fuss. I don't want the person to feel uncomfortable. And repel any offers to replace it—it was an accident. We love our things, but they're just things, after all.

Dinner parties have a life of their own. If my guests are having fun, we linger at the table, then move to the drawing room or the library for an after-dinner drink and more spirited conversation.

The Return of the Cocktail Party

When I was a young adult, a cocktail party was *the* place to be. Cocktail parties were sophisticated, glamorous, and populated by Beautiful People behaving outrageously. Wasn't *Breakfast at Tiffany's* a documentary? One of the best suggestions I can give to my younger readers is to bring back the cocktail party. To be clear, a cocktail party is something you host in your home during an appointed time frame—let's say 6–8 p.m. Guests are invited for drinks and conversation, with a few nibbles thrown in to offset too much drunken abandon (a little is fine). Here's why I think the cocktail party should be revived:

◈ Young people spend too much time and money in bars and clubs where they can't see, hear, or afford the overpriced drinks they order. A house party is more intimate.

◈ You can cast a wide net when you invite guests over for cocktails, increasing the chances that the "more" will end up being the "merrier." Try calling each person before you resort to sending the less personal

169

e-vite. And don't worry about space. People are friendlier when they stand very close together.

◈ A cocktail party at home can be inexpensive to mount—I'm all for that margarita machine, a shaker full of martinis, a pitcher of the house drink (the one you made up right before the party), a selection of well-priced wines, or all of the above. Want to dazzle your guests? Offer them whimsical cloth cocktail napkins with their drinks. They don't have to be expensive.

◈ The simple fact that you initiate such a retro event will establish you as a first-rate host or hostess who actually knows how to give a party. Maintain the image by planning the evening in advance—how many glasses, how many napkins, how many drinks per person, how much Chex mix or onion dip?

◈ If your home allows, set up a permanent bar with a few bottles, a decanter, glasses, and a cocktail shaker on a tray or side table. It will serve the same purpose as the three bars in my house. Add ice, garnishes, and nuts when you're expecting guests.

◈ It would be nice if your friends would reciprocate with invitations to their cocktail parties, but even if they don't, host yours at least once a year, around the holidays. People will campaign to get invited.

Obviously, the size of your guest list depends on how much space you have. I usually invite forty or fifty people for big cocktail parties, more if we're outside. The best time slot for cocktails is from 6–8 p.m., when the evening is young and people are fresh and bright. As for the dress code…if the party takes place during the holidays, people enjoy dressing up in festive "cocktail attire." At other times, "business attire" is fine.

I want to make sure that everyone is well fed, so I put out plenty of food, savory and sweet. My menu is usually the same, with a few variations. I serve assorted tea sandwiches, deviled eggs, a big bowl of shrimp on ice, ham on biscuits, cheese straws, celery stuffed with pimento cheese (a Southern favorite), and a beautiful cheese platter. I know what I like and I know exactly how it should be prepared and served, even if I rely on a caterer to do it for me. You may choose to make your own food (I've included several recipes), but if you have any intention of enjoying your own party, consider hiring a waiter and a bartender—the one extravagance that is absolutely worth it.

I've known Katie Lee, culinary personality, Food Network and Cooking Channel star, and the author of *The Endless Summer Cookbook* and *The Comfort Table*, for thirteen years. She learned true Southern cooking from her Grandma Dora while growing up in rural West Virginia, and she really knows how to host a party!

ASK THE EXPERT

Katie Lee

You grew up in the South; what dishes, or "comfort foods," are most vivid in your memory?

Some of my earliest memories are from my grandma's

On the piazza with the lovely Katie Lee.

kitchen. I loved making biscuits with her when I was a little girl. She would pull a stool over to the counter, and I would climb up and pat out the dough. I just loved them. She made the best sausage gravy and would ladle it over the biscuits. Whenever I want to feel close to her, or if I'm homesick, I'll just make a big batch of her biscuits.

In your experience, what recipe—especially something Southern— is a showstopper with guests?

Everyone loves deviled eggs at a cocktail party. My friends have come to expect them, and if I don't make any, I will hear about it. I like to use different garnishes, depending on the occasion. If we are having a more formal evening, I will spoon a little caviar on top, or if it is a casual Sunday evening, a small piece of bacon. People always go nuts for fried chicken, too. You can never go wrong with fried chicken.

Southern food sometimes has a reputation for being unhealthy— is there a way to update the old favorites so they don't break the calorie bank?

I look back and wonder how we weren't all as big as a house with the food we used to eat. It is easy to make a few adjustments, though, to make Southern food not quite as fattening. If I want the crunch of fried food without all of the fat, I will bread chicken or fish with crushed cornflakes, then bake. It isn't exactly the same, but it does the trick. I am not a fan of low-fat mayonnaise, so for mayonnaise-based salads, I use half regular mayo and half Greek yogurt. Instead of a ham hock in my collard greens, I use garlic and a little soy sauce. Buy a gravy separator; it's an easy way to skim off some of the fat and not lose any flavor.

Food presentation can be so important when entertaining—do you have any quick tricks for making food look really appetizing?

I am a big fan of serving classic comfort foods on my best china. People love simple foods and you can easily make them look really special. Meatloaf takes on a new life when served on a formal plate at a table that is perfectly set. Take the time to set your table the night before your dinner party, light candles, make a beautiful centerpiece, and the food will shine.

Young singles keep asking me for romance advice. What menu is guaranteed to win a heart? And does it involve chocolate cake?

A homemade meal is definitely the way to anyone's heart. In my personal experience, men love red meat. I think it is primal. Make him a big ribeye and he will do anything you want. Sear it in an iron skillet, baste it with butter, herbs, and garlic, then finish it in the oven. They also go nuts for warm chocolate chip cookies. Make the dough in advance, then bake them just before serving. The house will smell incredible, and nothing beats a warm chocolate chip cookie.

For a cocktail party, I have a large floral arrangement in the living room. But I tend to do something less traditional on the table in the butler's pantry. For example, I have an amazing Buddha that attracts a lot of attention. And we found a huge statue of Jack Daniel down south—I put him out when we do a cocktail party because I think he's amusing—at least he is to me.

When I'm confident that everything is ready, I enjoy the momentary quiet before my guests arrive. This is my time to put on my caftan, apply my makeup (which I call my "war paint"), sip my dressing drink, and do a final walk-through. I look at the way the food is laid out—some will be passed, some will be in the dining room, and the messiest food will stay in the butler's pantry—I don't want people eating barbecued chicken in the drawing room. Finally, I check the candles and rearrange the pillows.

At this point, the worst thing a guest can do is to arrive early. Michael will let them in, but they can just sit and stew until the official hour. At the other end of the rudeness spectrum are the people who turn up at 8 p.m., just when the party is supposed to be ending. Your time is important, but your host/hostess's time is important too, especially when they have gone to the trouble to entertain you.

Once the party begins, I dedicate myself to greetings, making introductions, rescuing wallflowers, and discreetly watching to see that glasses are refilled and hors d'oeuvres are circulating. Keep your pets away from the food if they're anything like Jaws, one of our beloved family dogs and a legend in his own time.

Jaws came to us when a friend of Whitney's offered us a puppy from his basset hound's litter. How could we refuse? He was adorable. But he never stopped teething and chewing on everything! It was 1975, and we had just seen the movie *Jaws* and noticed the similarities between the shark and our new dog, hence the name. We marveled at the way our Jaws could eat anything and everything: paper towel rolls, mail, a block of cheese from a cheese tray…

Jaws, the superstar of dogs, with Whitney.

At one memorable party, Jaws yanked a Smithfield ham from a serving table and dragged it behind a Chinese decorative screen. We could hear him chewing on it, but no one had the nerve to get close enough to take it away because he was growling while he was eating. The ham was so salty that, eventually, poor Jaws had to come out for water. When he did, we grabbed the remains. He drank constantly for a week—even from the toilet bowl.

But that's not the worst thing Jaws did at a cocktail party. Another night when I was hosting a party in honor of a famous senator, he got into one of the guest rooms, ransacked a suitcase, and swallowed a **diaphragm**. Then he came downstairs, made a lot of choking noises, and threw up the diaphragm in front of everybody, including the woman who owned it. There was a deadly silence. I reached for a napkin, deftly picked up the mess, and whisked it—and Jaws—out of the room. I guess it was a form of entertainment, because we talked about it for years to come.

> **Diaphragm:** a small rubber contraceptive dome.

After two hours of high-speed socializing, I'm ready to call it a night. I expect everyone to leave at the designated time, but if they don't, I have several foolproof ways of dealing with pesky stragglers. First, I turn off the music. Then I walk around the room with a candle snuffer in hand, gradually extinguishing the candles. The picture lights are next—I turn them off one by one. Finally, I start picking up the glasses—even the ones that people are still drinking. Once the room is dark and the alcohol has stopped flowing, most guests get the message (how observant!) and say goodnight. But there's always someone who foolishly believes you want the party to go on all night. That's when I say, "Do you need me to call you an Uber?" Or, "Can I walk you to your car?"

Everybody into the Pool (Especially Shep)

One of the benefits of living in the South is being able to entertain outside. I think that people today spend far too much time hunched over their smartphones and their iPads. They're so wrapped up in their work that it's important for them to be outdoors on occasion. One of my favorite things to do is to have a lawn party in the late afternoon, around 5:30 p.m. I have two small lawns here, so I set up badminton on one lawn and croquet on the other. And when I call people to invite them, I tell them that it's going to be really casual and to bring a bathing suit.

Now I'm going to share my best party tip of all time: rent a margarita machine. There's something about a frozen margarita that says "fiesta!" It's always a hit: when people are drinking margaritas, can a conga line be far behind? I usually get one from a party rental company, and I hire someone to accompany it and make the drinks, because the proportions can be tricky.

Second-best tip of all time: serve "poptails." I bought a book called *Poptails: Sixty Boozy Treats Served on a Stick*, by Erin Nichols, and discovered an absolutely brilliant thing: adult popsicles, or "poptails," including cosmopolitans, mint juleps, and dirty martinis. You mix the ingredients and pour them into special popsicle molds, so the alcohol freezes. They're refreshing, but with a kick.

In addition to serving margaritas and poptails, I fill a great big decorative clamshell with ice and stock it with bottles of beer, white wine, and rosé. I think that covers the party's alcohol component nicely. As for the menu, classic finger food never goes out of style. While people swim and play croquet, tea sandwiches are passed. There are two Southern classics that are my absolute favorites: white bread with homemade pimento cheese, and white bread with heirloom tomatoes, butter, salt, and pepper.

I always enjoy a good lawn party, but the South can get unbearably hot during the summer. Nobody ever, ever, entertains outdoors in August in the South. Remember my adage, "One cannot drink cheap wine in the heat." Not that I would serve cheap wine, but in August you should take a vacation or you should stay inside and read a book.

Even the most experienced hostesses have their brushes with disaster, especially if weather is a factor. Let me tell you about the party I almost didn't have. I'm always on the lookout for a fun theme if a party is going to be filmed for the show, because it makes it more visual. One day when Michael and I were out driving, we passed a hot-pink house on the beach. It was called Flamingo Manor, and it had statues of flamingos in the front. My first thought was to rent it for a party—I love flamingos and the color pink.

Whitney and I invited about two hundred people, many from out of the area. I came across some darling inflatable flamingos and ordered ten, not realizing that there were twelve in a package. When we put them in the pool it looked like a pink *Jurassic Park* (or as if Thomas Ravenel had been there). Of course, I had a stunning pink caftan at the ready. It's important for a hostess to look good and to feel comfortable, and a caftan takes care of both. I arranged for a caterer, a pink bar, a photographer, and a fortune teller. I think guests enjoy hearing predictions about the future, as long as they're lighthearted and optimistic.

The menu was my usual assortment of party favorites: tea sandwiches, ham biscuits, deviled eggs, sliced filet, and a fanciful dessert table with pink meringues and a pale pink cake. The pièce de résistance, I decided, would be an old-fashioned champagne tower. You don't see them much anymore, except at weddings. But I think they're beautiful and people are always fascinated by the way they work.

When you stack levels of champagne glasses—coupe, not flute—in precise configurations, and slowly pour champagne into the top glass, it magically flows into the glasses underneath. Get out your ruler and follow the directions below. You can tell your intellectual guests that this is a living illustration of trickle-down economics at its best.

If the idea of constructing a real champagne tower seems daunting to you, there is a way to cheat. Fill the glasses with pink champagne and stack them on Plexiglas trays—they'll look pretty standing there even if they don't do tricks.

After all of my careful party planning, everything seemed to be perfect. But in reality there is no such thing as perfection. The one thing you can count on is something going wrong. In this case, on the very Saturday of my party, Charleston was struck by a major hurricane—meteorologists predicted the worst rain in a thousand years. That says it all. The city flooded and much of it ended up under water. I don't know who had it worse, the out-of-town guests who were stuck en route because of the storm or the ones who managed to get here and were stranded.

The food had been delivered, so we had enough cocktail sandwiches and hors d'oeuvres to feed two hundred people. At first it seemed festive to indulge in so much party food, but after eating it for five days we couldn't look at finger foods or pink confections anymore.

Constructing a Champagne Tower

Y If you want to build the real thing, you will need a substantial table to use as the base, old-fashioned coupe champagne glasses, and a quantity of champagne.

Y First, calculate how many guests you want to serve. The number of glasses will determine how much champagne you need.

Y Let's say you have thirty guests, thirty glasses— each bottle of champagne fills about five glasses, so you will need six bottles for the first round. It may be easier to use three magnums. Oh, and open all the champagne before you start pouring.

Y Look at this process as a straightforward math problem. When you start building, the bottom level will consist of sixteen glasses laid out in a 4×4 square, with the glasses touching.

Y The next level will consist of nine glasses laid out in a 3×3 square. The stem of each glass should be centered over the diamond openings in the layer below.

Y The next level will consist of four glasses laid out in a 2×2 square.

Y And the final level is one glass placed at the center of the four below.

Y When the glasses are in place, and all eyes on are you, slowly pour champagne into the top glass and watch it trickle down. Keep pouring until all the glasses are full and your guests are suitably impressed by your magic powers.

Did we lose heart? Not at all. We bounced right back after the storm. I ordered the exact same food for the following weekend, and rounded up as many of the guests as possible (some of the out-of-towners couldn't make it). The biggest problem was that Flamingo Manor was unusable after the storm. At the last minute, I had to use my own backyard. We put the flock of inflated flamingos into the pool and started construction on the champagne tower.

The most important thing is not to get upset—be resilient. Even if the party is not exactly what you imagined, even if your best-laid plans are undermined, if you move ahead and have a good time, your guests will too. And my guests thoroughly enjoyed the Flamingo Party: The Sequel as much as they would have enjoyed the original.

Cameran showed up wearing a hot-pink dress and a flamingo on her head, and she's the only one who could pull off that look. Shep was especially dapper in a shocking pink tuxedo shirt, but what was really shocking was his pink flamingo Speedo, which he unveiled when he stripped down to his skivvies and jumped into the pool. Then Cameran fell into the bushes. Some of the Charmers can get pretty wild, and that's what keeps life interesting. And the fortune teller, bless her heart, told me I was rich.

I love this whimsical illustration of my Flamingo party by the artist Leslie Carrier.

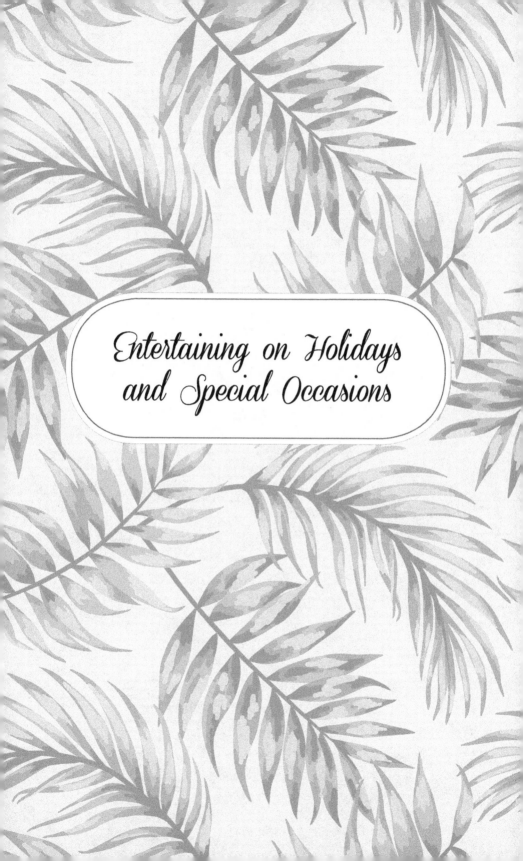

Entertaining on Holidays and Special Occasions

THE SOUTH DOESN'T HAVE SNOW LIKE THE CLASSIC "CHRISTMAS in Connecticut" tableau in the North, but we still go all out for the holiday. Another basic difference between Northerners and Southerners is that Northerners tend to go away in December. Arthur and I always headed for warm places during the holidays. But Southerners stay home, which means we decorate like crazy with magnolia leaves, holly berries, boxwood, and all those greens that are indigenous to the South. And, like our sociable ancestors, we entertain wildly. We enjoy a busy season of cocktail parties and open houses, going from home to home, spreading (and imbibing) good cheer.

The holiday season begins with the tree, which, in my house, is delivered the day after Thanksgiving. Fresh, of course, because the smell of fir is a major part of the Christmas experience. I really don't care for designer Christmas trees—the ones with special color schemes or coordinated decorations. They have no heart or soul and look as if they belong in a department store. This is the time to get really personal—to emphasize family and build traditions.

Cherish any decorations from previous generations, whether or not you like them. I have ornaments that belonged to my grandparents and red glass balls my mother bought that were on my very first Christmas tree. I also have ornaments that Whitney made as a child, and some that he bought for me. It still makes

Christmas with Whitney—my favorite way to spend the holiday, then and now.

me laugh to see the mermaid with exposed breasts he gave me when he was a teenager. He thought he was getting away with murder by putting something so risqué on the tree.

I love to buy antique ornaments at auction, especially if they're nineteenth-century Dresden and made of molded paper. In addition to my newly acquired elephant and among others, I have a beautifully crafted pug dog with a stick in his mouth. Whether an ornament is an antique, a collectible, or a family treasure, I value it because it holds a memory or tells a story, and I enjoy reliving these moments every time I decorate my tree.

While there's no right or wrong way to trim a tree, here are a few practical tips: If you have a very large tree topper, as I do—I have a giant peacock with a sweeping tail on the top of my very tall tree (doesn't everybody?)—the best way to attach it is to do so before the tree is set up. Use wire to secure the ornament, whether it's a star, a bird, or something else that strikes your fancy, then position the tree in its stand.

Next, put on the lights. This year I switched to LED lights. They're not quite as charming as the old lights, but they are safer. LED lights don't get hot, they don't dry out the tree, and you can leave them on for long periods of time.

There's a method to the way I hang my ornaments. I put the antiques and the family heirlooms in prominent places—then I fill in with the new (and sometimes wacky) ones. I add red or gold beads, which I end up throwing at the tree where I can't reach, but somehow it ends up looking fine. When I have a lot of time, I like to add strands of popcorn or cranberries.

When I'm finished with the tree, I start assembling the menagerie that has been a family tradition since Whitney was a child. He had several Winnie-the-Pooh stuffed animals he loved. My mother, who could make anything, knitted Christmas hats for them and they were given a place of honor on a little chair by the tree. I have added a few toys from my own childhood (which are now considered rare antiques), including a French Growler and a beautiful stuffed giraffe.

A few years ago, I rescued a camel from a thrift shop. It was made in the 1940s and used to be a part of a nativity scene, but it had been abandoned and was sitting on a shelf, dusty and forgotten. I brought it home and it sits in front of my tree, waiting for the arrival of a wise man, just like me.

I can never resist a Steiff animal. Not only are they beautifully made and incredibly lifelike, but they have a wonderful history. Margarete Steiff was a German seamstress who suffered from polio as a child. Despite the fact that she could use only one hand, she learned to sew. A stuffed fabric elephant—a pincushion, actually—was her first creation, followed by bears and

That face!

the other Steiff toys we love today. Her motto was, "Only the best is good enough for children."

It wouldn't be Christmas without my mechanical toys. I started my kitschy collection years ago with the iguana who sings "Feliz Navidad," and I just kept going. I have dogs, a flamingo, and a flower pot that belts out "Rockin' around the Christmas Tree." I gave one of these pots to an English friend who carried it home on the plane. Every time there was turbulence, I'm told, the pot started singing. I imagine it was a memorable flight.

The stockings are hung by the chimney with care: my mother needlepointed exquisite ones for the family, and each dog has one hanging from the fireplace in the kitchen. I also decorate the outside of the house with fresh garlands and wreaths. Williamsburg wreaths are very popular here in the South, and their distinguishing feature is that they're adorned with fruit. When I have time and I'm feeling creative, I make them myself. It reminds me of my childhood Christmases in Virginia.

I also enjoy the Christmassy fragrance of pomander balls and the *Nutcracker* look of sugared fruit. They are easy to make at home as well.

Williamsburg Wreath

Buy a fir wreath and several apples, pears, lemons, and a pineapple. Cut the pineapple in half, from top to bottom. Position the fruit on the wreath, pineapple halves on the bottom, and secure with strong, flexible wire. They're fun to make, but if you want something more professional, Williamsburg wreaths can be ordered from **ColonialWilliamsburg.com**.

Pomander Balls

Start with a firm orange, and use a nut pick to make tiny holes. Insert whole cloves in the holes, covering the orange.

Mix 1 teaspoon ground cinnamon, 1 teaspoon ground cloves, 1 tablespoon ground nutmeg, and 1 tablespoon allspice. Add ¼ cup powdered orris root (available from a pharmacy). Roll the orange in the mix and let it sit for a week, turning daily. Tie with a festive red ribbon and enjoy the scent!

Sugared Fruit

Assemble an assortment of fruit, including strawberries, pears, apples, and grapes. Wash and dry thoroughly.

Brush each piece with a thin layer of egg white and dust with extra-fine granulated sugar.

Place on waxed paper to dry—it usually takes about four hours.

They look good enough to eat, but they work best as holiday decorations, especially when displayed on a silver dish.

It takes about two days to finish putting up the Christmas decorations—and that's with help. Just in case you think I'm too traditional, I bought an inflatable Santa wearing camouflage at Walmart. I also have a replica of Graceland that plays Elvis's greatest hits. It's all about the high and the low!

When it comes to presents, I sidestep the drama and rush by shopping all year round. I have a large closet with a lock and key that becomes Santa's workshop—if I see a great gift for someone on my list I buy it and put it away. Remember to be generous to the people who do things for you all year. I also stock up on hostess gifts that might come in handy during the holidays. Béquet Confections makes the world's best salted caramels. I order twelve boxes, tie them with festive plaid ribbons, and I'm never empty-handed. Another wonderful gift is a Smithfield ham from Edwards, a family business founded in 1926. There's nothing better than a soft, white bread sandwich with lots of mayo and slices of genuine Smithfield ham.

We enjoy the spectacle until the first week in January, then it's time for the Christmas decorations and toys to go back into storage for the year. I have special boxes with individual compartments for ornaments that I bought at the Container Store. Remember to remove the batteries from anything that uses them—they can leak and destroy the mechanism. I've learned to be very organized about this process. However, despite my best efforts, the occasional box of ornaments still turns up under a bed.

Easter

I celebrate Easter with a special lunch after church, and I confess that there is nothing tasteful about my table on this holiday. The best way to describe it is high **kitsch**. I pile mounds of bunny grass—the kind you put in Easter baskets— and top them with papier-mâché rabbits. I also have glitter bunnies from Pottery Barn, bunnies pulling carts of candy (fancy candy and the drugstore variety, because I love them equally), Peeps, jelly beans, colored eggs, and alligator cookies with pink and yellow ribbons. There's barely room for plates and silverware.

Kitsch: art, objects, or design considered to be in poor taste because of excessive garishness or sentimentality, but sometimes appreciated in an ironic or knowing way.

When I'm feeling really playful, I put a trail of black jelly beans near each cottontail, signifying you-know-what. It adds that certain something.

The menu on Easter is Southern all the

way. I serve Smithfield ham with bourbon sauce, sweet potato soufflé, and *haricots verts*. The parade of bunnies continues at dessert, when we have a bunny cake (baked in a special bunny mold) covered with white frosting and coconut.

Horse Sense for a Kentucky Derby Party

I've had a lifelong love of horses, so I really enjoy celebrating the Kentucky Derby with my friends. The Derby, which takes place every May, gives me an opportunity to trot out all of my Southern favorites, from cocktails to desserts. Since I've hosted this event so many times, I'm going to use it to illustrate my timeline—and my choices—for a party that's off to the races.

I start the process in March. That's when I contact a caterer and send out handwritten invitations—no emails, ever! Guests are invited from 6 to 8 p.m., and they are asked to wear "Derby attire," which means that most men will show up in a seersucker suit and a bow tie, while most women will wear a white, or a pastel, dress.

I plan a menu that includes my favorite finger foods: ham biscuits, crustless tea sandwiches, deviled eggs, and a shrimp tower (my rule is nothing that's squishy, drippy, or red), and I rely on my caterer to prepare the dishes just the way I like them. I always provide my own trays and platters, so the food looks more personal. If you are a good cook, you can use my recipes (starting on page 193).

A Kentucky Derby party calls for the very best Southern cocktails. I serve authentic mint juleps in silver julep cups (any other presentation is blasphemous!), and *my* version of General Lee's artillery punch. General Lee's version, which involved

Mint Julep

A classic mint julep has four ingredients—mint, sugar, bourbon, and crushed ice—and must be served in a silver mint julep cup. Andy Cohen served them in mugs at one of the *Southern Charm* reunions. Yankees just don't get it!

- 4 mint leaves, plus more for garnish
- 1–2 teaspoons sugar, depending on how sweet you want it to be
- 2 ounces bourbon
- Crushed ice

In a silver mint julep cup, tear up mint. Add sugar and a small splash of bourbon. Muddle until mint leaves are pulpy. Add bourbon, and stir until sugar dissolves. Top with ice (which you have crushed in a Lewis bag with a mallet), and garnish with mint sprig.

mixing any alcohol the soldiers could find in a horse bucket, is disgusting and will make everyone sick.

Praised (or condemned, depending on your point of view) as the "strongest drink in America," General Lee's (or Chatham) artillery punch is an historic drink that can leave you with an historic hangover. Whitney made it in a haphazard way at one *Southern Charm* party, throwing in everything but the kitchen sink. When he asked one of the guests how it tasted, they answered, "Drunk!" Even the Southern reprobates wouldn't drink it.

If you don't want your guests passing out on the living room floor, serve this lethal drink in punch cups, which are smaller than glasses. And ladle judiciously!

General Lee's Artillery Punch

- 3 teaspoons fresh lemon juice
- 2 cups superfine sugar
- 1 pint bourbon
- 1 pint cognac
- 1 pint dark Jamaican rum
- 3 bottles good-quality champagne

Mix alcohol with lemon juice and sugar and let sit in the refrigerator for twenty-four hours to mellow it out. When ready to serve, pour over a block of ice in a punch bowl and top with thinly cut slices of orange and small strawberries. Then, watch what happens live!

Check in advance to make sure you have proper glassware, in the right quantities. You can rent silver mint julep cups and a punch bowl and punch cups if you don't own them.

I have fun with the dessert at this party. I serve sugar cookies shaped like horses. Their manes and tales are frosted, as are their neckpieces. I also have frosted horseshoe cookies. They look adorable on platters, and they make great party favors. It's a Southern thing to place little bags of them at the door for people to take home.

I know I usually sound like the queen of kitsch, but on this occasion, I like to keep the décor simple. Roses are nice, because the race's nickname is "A Run for the Roses." I like to position food and drink in various places around the house so guests can move freely. Finally, I know this may be hard for you, but never surrender to the temptation to use paper napkins. Linen ones make a guest feel special.

Patricia's Party Recipes

Tea sandwiches are better in the South because we have a secret ingredient: Duke's mayonnaise. Duke's was born in 1917, when Mrs. Eugenia Duke whipped it up in her sandwich shop in Greenville, South Carolina. It has been the unofficial mayonnaise of the South ever since then. If you don't have a local Piggly Wiggly, you can locate a store that carries Duke's at **dukesmayo.com**, or you can order it online. Duke's will make any recipe taste authentically Southern.

Basically, all tea sandwiches are made the same way. Trim the crusts off slices of Wonder Bread (or another soft white bread—or even a healthy one!), spread with your favorite filling, and cut the sandwiches diagonally, or use a cookie cutter to make shapes.

Cucumber Sandwiches

- Cucumber, peeled and thinly sliced
- A pinch of garlic salt
- A pinch of fresh dill weed, finely chopped
- Butter (we use *real* butter in the South, not something that tastes like butter)
- Duke's mayonnaise

Spread butter on one slice of Wonder Bread and Duke's mayo on the other. Cover the buttered side with sliced cucumber, a pinch of garlic salt, and a pinch of dill weed. Top with the mayonnaised slice to make a sandwich. Cut diagonally.

Tomato Sandwiches

An authentic Southern tomato sandwich barely needs a recipe. Remove crusts from Wonder Bread and cut into circles with a cookie cutter or a biscuit cutter. Spread with Duke's mayonnaise. Slice a ripe tomato (preferably in season), sprinkle with a tiny bit of salt, let sit on paper towels to get rid of the oozy stuff, and place between bread rounds.

Egg Salad

Y 8 eggs
Y ½ cup Duke's mayonnaise
Y 1 teaspoon French's mustard
Y Salt and pepper to taste
Y Paprika

Hard boil eggs, then cool, peel, and chop them. Mix the chopped eggs with mayonnaise and mustard. Add salt and pepper to taste. Remove crusts from Wonder Bread and spread with egg salad. Sprinkle outer top with paprika. Cut diagonally.

Chicken Salad Sandwiches

Y 2 cups chopped, cooked organic chicken
Y ½ cup Duke's mayonnaise
Y ½ cup diced celery
Y ½ cup diced carrot
Y 1 ⅓ cup diced onion
Y 1 tablespoon yellow mustard
Y 1 teaspoon celery salt
Y Ground pepper to taste

Mix the ingredients in a bowl. Remove crusts from Wonder Bread and spread the chicken salad. Cut diagonally.

Ham Biscuits

I serve ham biscuits at most of my parties. This is another Southern specialty that is more of a conversation than a recipe. For the sliced ham, use Edwards Virginia ham whenever possible. For the biscuits…well, you can buy them from a bakery or use frozen. If you want to make your own, a basic buttermilk biscuit recipe is best.

- 2 cups flour
- 4 teaspoons baking powder
- ¼ teaspoon baking soda
- 2 tablespoons Crisco
- ¾ teaspoon salt
- 2 tablespoons butter
- 1 cup buttermilk

Preheat oven to 450 degrees. Mix flour, baking powder, baking soda, and salt in a bowl. Add Crisco and butter until batter reaches a crumbly consistency. Add buttermilk and stir until dough forms. Place the dough on a floured surface and dust with flour. Fold the dough into itself several times and form a round that's about an inch thick. Use a biscuit cutter to cut individual biscuits. Line up on a cookie sheet. Bake fifteen to twenty minutes, until golden. When the biscuits have cooled, slice them open, put the ham in the biscuit, and there you go!

Pimento Cheese, the "caviar" of the South

I love pimento cheese, and so does everyone else. Whip up a bowl and serve it on celery (my favorite), on crackers, or on Wonder Bread, tea sandwich style.

- 8 ounces good quality, extra-sharp cheddar cheese, freshly grated
- ½ cup softened cream cheese
- ½ cup jarred pimento
- 4 tablespoons Duke's mayonnaise
- Pinch garlic powder
- Salt and pepper to taste

Mix all ingredients by hand in a bowl until smooth. Use any way you like, or refrigerate in a tight-lidded container. Pimento cheese will stay fresh for about a week.

Caramelized Bacon

Sinfully delicious and a party favorite.

- Thick center-cut bacon
- Dark brown sugar

Preheat oven to 350 degrees. Press individual bacon strips in brown sugar until coated on both sides. Place on a rack and bake until brown and crispy. Remove and drain on the rack.

I once made the mistake of using a paper towel to remove the excess fat and the paper stuck to the bacon (oddly enough, that didn't prevent anyone from eating it). Cut each strip into thirds and serve on a platter. Watch it disappear!

Festive Herbed Nuts

- 1 teaspoon kosher salt
- Pinch of fresh black pepper
- ¼ teaspoon cayenne pepper
- 2 heaping teaspoons dark brown sugar
- 1 heaping teaspoon finely chopped fresh rosemary leaves
- 1 ½ tablespoons melted butter
- 2 tablespoons olive oil
- 4 cups pecan halves

Preheat oven to 350 degrees. Place pecans in a baking dish and bake for fifteen minutes—careful, they burn quickly! Combine cooked pecans with the other ingredients in a baggie and shake like crazy until the nuts are coated evenly. Serve in a pretty dish.

A Good Ol' Southern Crab Feast

The only time I will go to someone's house and eat in their kitchen is if they're serving a traditional crab feast—then I'm happy to do so! This is a messy meal that requires a utilitarian setting—either a table in the kitchen or one out-of-doors. And make sure the table is not made of glass, or you will be sorry.

First you cover the table with newspaper, bring out the hammers, crab crackers, and picks, and pound the crab to remove the succulent meat from its shell. Add melted butter, lemon wedges, and corn on the cob. And, for dessert, an old-fashioned, soda parlor root beer float. You will need a bath when you're finished, but this meal is absolute heaven! Peel-and-eat shrimp can be fun when crab (best served July through November) is out of season.

How to Prepare Crabs for a Crab Feast

- Y 1 cup cider
- Y 1 bottle of beer
- Y ½ cup Old Bay seasoning
- Y 1 dozen live blue crabs
- Y Pinch of salt

Crabs are best cooked in a steamer. Mix the beer, cider, and 2 tablespoons of Old Bay with 1 ½ cups water and simmer in the bottom of the steamer pot. Place the crabs in the steamer insert, making sure they do not touch the water. Sprinkle the remaining Old Bay and salt on each layer of crabs. Cover and steam for thirty minutes. When they're completely orange, they're done.

The Hostess Gift— Go Beyond the Candle

I LOVE GIVING (AND RECEIVING) CLEVER HOSTESS GIFTS. SOME require a little more advance thought—but not much. And there are gifts that can be stockpiled, so you're always prepared to be the best guest. These gifts work for me every time:

◈ See's Candy (**sees.com**). Have you figured out that I have a sweet tooth?

◈ Lewis ice bag and mallet—this heavy-grade natural canvas bag is the best medium for crushing ice for a cocktail. You can find it in many stores as well as at Amazon, and it is usually sold with a wooden mallet.

◈ Shutterfly (**shutterfly.com**) is a great source for gifts customized with photographs. Postage stamps, playing cards, wrapping paper, puzzles—a beautiful or whimsical photograph can turn an everyday item into a source of delight. Recently I saw wrapping paper that was decorated with pictures of the family dogs!

◈ Cookie cutters with meaning—you can get any shape online at **cookiecutters.com.**

◈ Leontine Linens (**leontinelinens.com**) makes a beautiful quilted lingerie bag that can be monogrammed.

◈ Sabatino truffles (**sabatinotruffles.com**) for the fabulous gift of a truffle and a truffle shaver. Other gift items include beautifully packaged truffle salt, truffle oil...all things truffle!

◈ For beautiful custom Christmas tree ornaments contact Kathe Knitch (**sweetruin.etsy.com**). She also makes masks that are works of art (for that masked ball you have to go to, or just because...).

◈ Béquet Confections (**bequetconfections.com**) for the world's best salted caramels. Buy several boxes... and hide them from yourself!

◈ Smithfield ham from Edwards (**edwardsvaham. com**) because there's nothing better than a soft white bread sandwich with lots of Duke's mayo and Smithfield ham.

My Life Right Now

Pet Tales

I think pets are life-enhancing. My doctors at the Mayo Clinic say that sleeping with an animal enables you to get a better night's rest and that petting an animal lowers your blood pressure. Pets are great companions. They give you unconditional love. They are fascinating on so many levels; I find them fun and amusing, especially when they do silly things.

At the moment, I have five dogs in residence: Siegfried and Roy, who are Pomeranians; Monty, the truffle dog; Smoochy, Whitney's boxer; and Chauncey, our baby pug. As Whitney says, life here is "a little of *Downton Abbey* and a lot of *Animal House*." Thank God that Michael adores the dogs and treats them like beloved children. They are the heart and soul of the house and each one has a personality—and a story—all his/her (Smoochy's a girl) own.

Smoochy (top) and Chauncey.

There are dogs I have loved and lost. Jaws, of course, still lives in legend because he was always getting into one kind of crazy trouble or another. When we lived in Washington, a friend of mine started a high-end jewelry line. I invited other friends to come for lunch and to see her collection and do some private shopping. When we were finished with our lovely meal, we went to the living room—and it looked as if the house had been robbed! Leather pouches were strewn all over the place and, shockingly, a valuable sapphire-and-diamond ring was missing. There, in the middle of the mess, was a very guilty dog—Jaws, the jewel thief!

I rushed him to the vet to see what we could do. An X-ray confirmed that he had swallowed the ring and, unfortunately, there was only one way to get it back. I had to feed him mountains of Wonder Bread, walk him every four hours, and use a plastic fork to search through his output for the ring. I always wondered what the neighbors were thinking. It took three days for it to work its way through his system. I was disgusted by the whole process and a little worried about the condition of the ring. But after we dipped it in jewelry cleaner it looked as good as ever.

Jaws would eat anything, and that proved to be his downfall. Years after the ring incident, Whitney and I were summering in Malibu when Jaws swallowed a golf ball. We tried everything, including surgery, but the poor pup didn't make it.

Lily was my first pug, and she came into my life in an unexpected way. When I was living in New York, I made the mistake of stopping into a pet store (aka a puppy mill, which I didn't know at the time) with a friend of mine. While we were playing with the puppies, I spotted a mischievous little pug racing all over the place, creating havoc. I had to buy her—she was *that* cute—and that was Lily. She was the sweetest dog, and I adored her. But because she came from a puppy mill, she was plagued with all kinds of medical problems and she ultimately went blind.

Eventually I had to carry Lily everywhere. She was so heavy that one day I almost fell down the stairs with her in my arms. After she passed away in 2013, I decided that the next addition to my dog menagerie would be small and portable. Ordinarily, I rescue my pets—over the years, I've rescued at least twenty, including dogs, cats, and horses. But this time I set out to find a breeder and my research led me to Florida, where the person who had been named breeder of the year maintained a kennel.

Soon I was off on a road trip to the Tampa area to pick up an adorable Pomeranian puppy. Actually, make that two adorable Pomeranian puppies. I heard from the breeder that two brothers—one black, one white—had bonded, and I didn't think it would be right to separate them. That's how I ended up with Siegfried and Roy.

Michael holding Siegfried (L) and Roy (R).

Once I was in the state of Florida, I had to stop to visit an animal from my childhood. The South Florida Museum in Bradenton is home to Snooty the Manatee, the world's oldest manatee living in captivity. Snooty came to the museum in 1949 and was quite an attraction, so not long after he arrived, my parents brought me to see him. What an impression he made on me when I was a child! Now, all these years later, I was touched to see him again, because he brought back memories of my mother and father and the wonderful times we shared in Florida. I feel a real connection to Snooty, who celebrated his sixty-eighth birthday not long ago.

Our dog family expanded with the arrival of sweet Smoochy, who lived with Whitney in Los Angeles, and Toby, a rescue dog who was found tied up in a back yard, loaded with buckshot. Toby was such a love. I adopted him, had the buckshot removed, and gave him his very first toy and, I hope, a happy life, though he's sadly passed away now. We also had Nyla, Michael's dog. In 2013, we welcomed Monty, the Lagotto, a breed that specializes in hunting truffles, although I haven't trained Monty to do that. It's probably a waste of a great talent.

When Lily died, I really missed having a pug, so that's when Chauncey came into our lives. Chauncey has won everyone's heart; one look at his little face makes the day better. We dress him in outfits (which are always a little snug), and watch him play sidekick to Monty, who is three times his size.

While we were going to the dogs, we also had cats. My Siamese cats Kitty Kelly and Rambo moved to New York with me when I married Arthur, and I had two rescue cats, Rhett and Ashley. Then there was Rocky, a beautiful Himalayan, who passed away last year. He was the last animal Arthur and I picked out together—he was advertised in a local newspaper in Connecticut—and he was devoted to Arthur. When Arthur got sick, Rocky stayed on his bed all the time.

It was only after Arthur died that Rocky started sleeping with me—I miss him because he always made me think of

Rocky

Michael holding Monty.

Arthur. I have a little pet cemetery by the side of the house where many of our dogs and cats are buried.

Growing up, I always had dogs, cats, and horses. I believe animals enhance your life in every way and I cannot imagine life without them. When we tape the show sometimes one of my dogs runs into a scene, and I just pick him up and sit him on the chair next to me. It's fun to watch their antics. For example, last year we wanted to decorate Easter eggs. We boiled a dozen, set them out on a tea towel to cool, and walked away for a few minutes. Monty, with the help of several of his four-legged coconspirators, pounced. He pulled the towel from the table and ate all the eggs—shells on!

When I was growing up, our pets were happy with table scraps and never once went to a vet. Now, of course, my dogs are on high-end diets and they see their vet so often that he's become a family friend. I remember taking Jaws to a vet in Beverly Hills who was in a big facility with other animal physicians with **esoteric** specialties. There were signs for everything from canine reproduction to bird orthodontia. I've always said that if I ever needed a hysterectomy this is where I would go—the pet hospital in Beverly Hills was the biggest and the best I've ever seen.

Esoteric: intended for or likely to be understood by only a small number of people with a specialized knowledge or interest.

There's no end to the treatments my pets need. Siegfried and Roy tried acupuncture for their knees. Rocky received daily dialysis until he died. Can a pet psychiatrist be far behind? My animals are expensive, but I regard them as my children and I'm happy to indulge them.

Or, as Whitney points out, "Mom takes her pets very seriously—she grew up with cats, dogs, parrots—and I think she compensates for not having grandkids by surrounding herself with tons of animals. Her house is like a Southern Grey Gardens." I'm not sure he meant it as a compliment, but I'll take it that way.

The Reality of Reality Television

Bravo launched *Southern Charm* with an appealing cast and an atmospheric location—beautiful, historic Charleston, the city *everyone* wants to see. My participation in the show was impromptu. Whitney decided that he wanted me to appear in one of the early episodes. The sound man mic'ed me up and I walked into my son's room while he was playing the guitar— something he does every day—and asked him to turn down his amplifier—something *I* do every day. There are times when the vibrations are so loud I can't hear myself think!

I noticed a pile of cheap clothes on the floor and learned that they belonged to Whitney's most recent "Southern sleepover." Instantly, my **acerbic** sense of humor kicked in. I forgot that the camera was there and said whatever popped into my head, and it was fun. It came as quite a surprise to me that I felt so at home on the show, because I've never enjoyed public speaking. When I received the woman of the year award for philanthropy, I got up and said only, "Thank you for this lovely award." That was it. People loved that my speech was so short.

Acerbic: sharp and forthright.

Like Alice falling through the rabbit hole, I entered the surreal world of Bravo reality television. Not that I knew much about reality shows. I watched Bravo for the first time when Whitney started producing *Southern Charm*. I gave all the *Housewives* a shot and found the Beverly Hills group the most amusing. I watched *Million Dollar Listing New York*, and it made me sad that I sold my New York apartment and house too soon, before the incredible real estate boom. And I watched the Kardashians, until one of them had her rear end lasered on television. That was the end for me—yes, pun intended.

I enjoy *Below Deck* because I spent two years on the "upper deck," when I was married to Ed Fleming. I know firsthand that there is ample drama below. We lost a deckhand who couldn't get along with the captain, and we were in Demopolis, Alabama, when we lost our cook—believe me, you're not going to find a new cook in Demopolis, Alabama. I had to prepare our meals until a replacement arrived. It was a nightmare.

I'm probably the last person who should be on a reality show but, gradually, I became a regular on *Southern Charm*. During the first season, it seemed that the more the Charmers misbehaved, the more I was asked to comment on their bad behavior. Then, and now, the "kids" use me as a sounding board. They tell me what they did and said, and I tell *them* what they did

wrong, and what they *should* have said. I'm like a surrogate mother, but the fun kind. I make snarky comments. I tease and chide them when they need it—which is frequently. I never fail to call them out when the opportunity arises, because I want them to be better. And I give them advice, whether or not they ask for it. I also serve the best cocktails in town.

I represent a more civilized way of life. Yes, I have standards, but I'm not a snob. And people seem to be genuinely interested in the way I live—the manners I take for granted, the clothes I wear, the way my home is decorated, and especially how I entertain.

People always ask me if the show is scripted. The answer is no. There's nothing that says "Charleston should get hit with a hurricane" or "Patricia should get a new dog." I like to have fun on camera. If appearing on a reality show meant that I had to take it seriously, I wouldn't do it. I am always my outspoken (and some would say outrageous) self, and I never lose sleep about how I'm portrayed. I just don't want them putting up any ugly pictures of me!

On a practical note, it's never a good idea to have your home invaded by a camera crew. All of that heavy equipment is difficult to control. On one occasion, a camera went through an eighteenth-century pane of glass. Then there was the time when a distracted camera operator backed up and broke an antique Irish decanter that belonged to my father. And I don't know who dropped what on my antique chair in the foyer, but it left a nasty impression. That said, the Bravo crew is always pleasant, polite, and considerate. In this house, of all places, it is hard not to be a bull in the china shop.

I find it interesting that so many different kinds of people watch *Southern Charm*. Men often tell me that they never, ever, saw a reality show until their wives got them hooked on this one. In my experience, *Southern Charm* fans are very friendly.

They're always pleasant and respectful when I run into them. Tourists come to see the house because it is so recognizable, and they wave to me when I'm sitting on my piazza. I walked into a hotel elevator the other day and an elderly couple screamed "It's you!" They had actually come to Charleston hoping for a spontaneous encounter, and they left with a selfie of the three of us.

Bumping into someone in Charleston is one thing, but I was on the other side of the world, in a gift shop in Jaipur, India, of all places, when I met a fan from San Francisco. People are surprised because they are just as likely to find me at Costco as at the Polo Bar in the Beverly Hills Hotel. I get around! It is a little embarrassing when you are trying to do something personal, like pick up a prescription, or when you don't look your best. Still, so far everyone has been lovely. I've never had anyone say "you're a cranky old bitch" (though I'm sure that day will come).

Initially, I think Michael was horrified by the thought of opening the house (and our lives, for that matter) to the outside world. He maintains that one of the advantages of being wealthy is having privacy. But he's the first to admit that "every domestic has a touch of the actor," and now he's performing on a very big stage! He jokes about getting his own agent.

Michael has quite a following and loves interacting with his fans. They greet him wherever he goes, and he's incredibly good-humored about it, especially if he has one of the dogs with him. He says that people want to know if I'm nice. They're probably disappointed when he answers yes.

We set up a "Have a question for Michael?" button on my website **PatriciaAltschul.com**, and it is so amusing to see the questions and comments that come in. There are the predictable inquiries about the best way to remove a stain from carpeting, or the brand of Michael's favorite silver polish. But there are also questions from left field, such as the time a fellow Charleston resident asked Michael about a random car that had been parked on our street for a few days. Apparently, Michael is supposed to know *everything*.

I have *Southern Charm* to thank for my expertise with the internet and social media. Before the show, I knew the basics—how to email and navigate Google—and believe me, I have friends who can't do either. Now, my desire to interact with fans has catapulted me into the unexplored worlds of Twitter and Instagram. The world is moving so fast that it is very important to be conversant in the latest modes of communication. I think it keeps me young, smart, and connected to pop culture.

Sometimes I look at my followers on Instagram and Twitter, and I can see from their pictures that they're all over the map. There are young girls, older men, couples, even dogs and cats. And some are hardcore fans who are devoted to the show and fiercely protective of the cast members they like. If someone posts something objectionable, they react instantly.

During the season, I get as many as five hundred tweets a night. I recognize all the regulars. Total engagement is important, so I often spend a few hours each day reading and responding. That's when it feels like a full-time job. What makes a good tweet? I try to say something personal. I thank people who are nice. And I retweet ones I enjoy, especially if they have to do with animals.

Instagram is more fun, in my opinion. The process of posting is straightforward, and we all know that a picture—or a video—is worth a thousand words. I have a good time putting up images of the dogs, Whitney, my Christmas tree, or the cast of *Southern Charm* (not necessarily in that order). And I enjoy my glimpses into other people's lives via their Instagram accounts.

Being me, I do have a few rules regarding proper behavior on social media and the internet:

◈ I don't want any negativity on any of my accounts. Isn't this supposed to be fun? I take great pleasure in blocking the worst offenders. I feel as if I am ridding the world of unpleasantness, one troll at a time.

◈ Don't give away too much personal information. Prospective employers always check social media.

◈ It can be dangerous to post pictures while you're on vacation—kind of like leaving your door at home unlocked.

◈ Don't engage with crazy people—it only encourages them to get crazier.

◈ Don't take anything personally.

I'm generally pretty good about letting internet insults roll off my back, except when bloggers insist that I am not Southern because I was born in Florida. Hmmm. Geography definitely needs to be revived in schools. The last time I looked at a map of the United States, Florida was in the South. And if we're talking about the **antebellum** South, Florida was the third of the seven states to secede from the Union and form the Confederacy. On top of that, I grew up in Virginia. So, who still wants to say I'm not from the South?

> **Antebellum:** occurring or existing before a particular war, especially the American Civil War.

I consider myself Southern from head to toe, but I'll let *you* decide whether or not I'm charming. I certainly am happy.

I've been working hard on the show, this book, and the caftan line I'm launching with Georgette. There's also

Whitney (and the family I hope he will have one day), the dogs, the house, and my friends. It takes a lot of effort to have a so-called charmed life, but if you get it right, it's worth every bit of time and trouble you put into it.

And, when it works, it truly *is* an art!

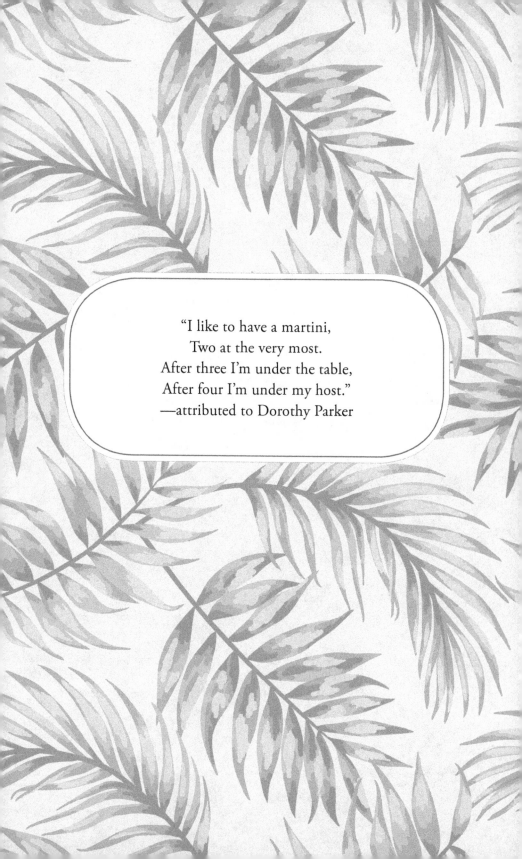

"I like to have a martini,
Two at the very most.
After three I'm under the table,
After four I'm under my host."
—attributed to Dorothy Parker

Acknowledgments

Patricia Altschul

I have been blessed in so many ways, and the greatest blessing of all is my son, Whitney Sudler-Smith. My thanks to him, and to my dear family and the many friends who have enabled me to enjoy such a wonderful life. I am especially grateful to the extraordinary Mario Buatta, Georgette Mosbacher, Carolyne Roehm, Katie Lee, Cathy Horyn, and Carson Kressley for their generous contributions to this book. Thank you Bravo, Kathleen French, Aaron Rothman, Jessica Chesler, my fellow cast members on *Southern Charm*, and the show's devoted fans—you are my extended family. Thanks also to John Paul Horstmann, Bobby Kenner, and Roeg Sutherland. At home, I depend on Michael Kelcourse and Joan DiPietro for everything, and I am thankful every day. I'd also like to acknowledge Luzanne Otte, Karen Thornton, and Madison LeCroy. And I extend my deepest appreciation to my friend and co-author, Deborah Davis, whose eloquent writing has brought my story to life.

Deborah Davis

I am grateful to my husband, Mark Urman, my mother, Jean Gatto, and my children, Cleo Davis-Urman, Oliver Davis-Urman, and Oliver's bride, Jessica Caroline Cox, for being such a loving and supportive family. I would also like to thank the wonderful team at Diversion—Jaime Levine, Nita Basu, Sarah Masterson Hally, and, of course, Scott Waxman, for their dedication and enthusiasm. Finally, my thanks to the one and only Patricia Altschul for turning work into play, and for teaching me all about charm and the magical powers of caftans and cocktails!

Patricia Altschul is the surprise breakout star of the Bravo hit reality series, *Southern Charm*, and has been featured in publications including *Vogue, Town and Country, Architectural Digest*, and *People*. Wise, cultivated, elegant, and funny, Patricia is a consummate hostess and a lifestyle icon whose unique combination of class *and* sass has endeared her to fans of all ages. Patricia has earned her status as a preeminent tastemaker. She received her Master's Degree from George Washington University, where she lectured on Art History, and was a highly successful art advisor who also amassed her own art collection. In addition to being an academic and a philanthropist, she has done a life-long tour-of-duty at the top of the social ladder in Washington, D.C., Oyster Bay, and on Manhattan's storied Fifth Avenue, where she observed—and ultimately dictated—the modern-day rules of civility. Patricia has a glorious brain, the best legs, and a killer sense of humor, and expertly curates every aspect of her life.

Instagram & Twitter: @pataltschul
Website: patriciaaltschul.com

Deborah Davis is the author of eight books, including *Strapless: John Singer Sargent and the Fall of Madame X*, *Party of the Century: The Fabulous Story of Truman Capote and His Black and White Ball*, *The Oprah Winfrey Show: Reflections on an American Legacy*, *Guest of Honor: Booker T. Washington, Theodore Roosevelt, and the White House Dinner that Shocked a Nation*, which won the prestigious Phillis Wheatley Award for best work of History in 2013, and *The Trip: Andy Warhol's Plastic-Fantastic Cross-Country Adventure*.

Instagram: @therealdeborahdavis